Writing Extra

A resource book of multi-level skills activities

CAMBRIDGE
UNIVERSITY PRESS

Graham Palmer

PUBLISHED BY THE PRESS SYNDICATE OF THE UNIVERSITY OF CAMBRIDGE
The Pitt Building, Trumpington Street, Cambridge, United Kingdom

CAMBRIDGE UNIVERSITY PRESS
The Edinburgh Building, Cambridge CB2 2RU, UK
40 West 20th Street, New York, NY 10011–4211, USA
477 Williamstown Road, Port Melbourne, VIC 3207, Australia
Ruiz de Alarcón 13, 28014 Madrid, Spain
Dock House, The Waterfront, Cape Town 8001, South Africa

http://www.cambridge.org

First published 2004

Printed in the United Kingdom at the University Press, Cambridge

Typefaces Congress Sans, Ulissa Rounded 9.5pt. *System* QuarkXPress®

A catalogue record for this book is available from the British Library

ISBN 0 521 53287 6

Contents

Map of the book

Theme	Title	Topic	Activity type	Writing focus	Time
1 Personal information					
Elementary	**1.1** Pickpocket!	identifying people, crime	group role play	form, statement	50 mins
Intermediate	**1.2** Who's who	identifying famous people	paired puzzle-solving, text analysis	biography	50 mins
Upper-intermediate	**1.3** Jobsearch	jobs	group game, role play, text analysis	CV (Curriculum Vitae)	50 mins
2 The family					
Elementary	**2.1** Dinner's in the oven	relationships, food	paired matching, text analysis	personal note	50 mins
Intermediate	**2.2** Trouble with the in-laws	marriage	group role play	personal letter (apology)	50 mins
Upper-intermediate	**2.3** Family matters …	genealogy	simulation	e-mail, register	50 mins
3 Daily activities					
Elementary	**3.1** Nothing happened today	routines, relationships	paired text analysis	diary entry, memoir	50 mins
Intermediate	**3.2** Prison: doing time	prison routines	paired text analysis	writing a report; editing for length	50 mins
Upper-intermediate	**3.3** Murder mystery	crime, alibis	paired puzzle-solving, role play	summary report, note taking	50 mins
4 Homes					
Elementary	**4.1** Designer kitchen	kitchens, good design	group problem-solving	report	50 mins
Intermediate	**4.2** Holiday house-swap	houses, holidays	matching, paired simulation	personal letter (descriptive); linking	50 mins
Upper-intermediate	**4.3** The student house	rules, communal living	group role play	rules	50 mins
5 Town and country					
Elementary	**5.1** Get lost!	directions, relationships	paired role play	personal letter (giving directions)	50 mins
Intermediate	**5.2** The news on the street	local newspapers	text analysis, group simulation	news article; expanding notes	50 mins
Upper-intermediate	**5.3** The big move	moving to the countryside	paired role play	personal letter (opinion); editing for emphasis	50 mins
6 Travel and tourism					
Elementary	**6.1** Wish you were here …	holiday problems	text analysis	postcard	50 mins
Intermediate	**6.2** Paradise tours	choosing package holidays	matching, text analysis	brochure description; targeting audience	50 mins
Upper-intermediate	**6.3** FAQs: Frequently Asked Questions	transport advice	paired text analysis	website; targeting audience	50 mins

Theme	Title	Topic	Activity type	Writing focus	Time
7 Food and drink					
Elementary	**7.1** A lovely meal	dinner parties	simulation	personal letter (descriptive)	50 mins
Intermediate	**7.2** The Greasy Spoon	restaurant hygiene	paired spot-the-difference, text analysis	report	50 mins
Upper-intermediate	**7.3** Black or white?	marketing coffee	group simulation	advertising copy; expanding notes	50 mins
8 Describing people					
Elementary	**8.1** Virtually friends	Internet friendships	matching, paired role play	personal e-mail	50 mins
Intermediate	**8.2** Business contacts	meeting business contacts	text analysis	business e-mail	50 mins
Upper-intermediate	**8.3** The shape of hands …	introducing characters	text analysis	fiction	50 mins
9 Describing things					
Elementary	**9.1** Internet bargains	personal belongings	whole class game	catalogue descriptions	50 mins
Intermediate	**9.2** It's a whatsit	everyday objects	group quiz	dictionary definitions	50 mins
Upper-intermediate	**9.3** Dream limo	custom limousines	paired simulation	fax; checking for meaning	50 mins
10 Friends and relationships					
Elementary	**10.1** Dear John …	crisis in a relationship	paired role play	personal letter (giving news)	50 mins
Intermediate	**10.2** Soap opera	new soap opera characters	paired simulation	feature article; expanding ideas	50 mins
Upper-intermediate	**10.3** Who gets the children?	pre-nuptial agreements	paired role play, text analysis	formal contract; adding punctuation	50 mins
11 Health and fitness					
Elementary	**11.1** More gain, less pain	encouraging healthy lifestyles	group text analysis	website feature article; expanding ideas	50 mins
Intermediate	**11.2** First Aid	emergency First Aid	paired text analysis, simulation	informative leaflet; editing for logic and focus	50 mins
Upper-intermediate	**11.3** The Donor Campaign	organ donor campaign	group simulation	TV advert storyboard	50 mins
12 Leisure time					
Elementary	**12.1** Leisure for all	planning a sports/leisure centre	group simulation	questionnaire	50 mins
Intermediate	**12.2** I win!	explaining board games	group board game	instructions, rules	50 mins
Upper-intermediate	**12.3** A really good read …	reviewing for a website	paired text analysis	reviews; correcting style and structure	50 mins

Map of the book

Theme	Title	Topic	Activity type	Writing focus	Time
13 Education					
Elementary	**13.1** A likely excuse …	excuses for absence	group board game	absence note	50 mins
Intermediate	**13.2** Writing class	the writing process	paired simulation	promotional flier; targeting audience	50 mins
Upper-intermediate	**13.3** Cyberstudy	virtual language schools	group discussion, text analysis	discursive composition; linking ideas	50 mins
14 The world of work					
Elementary	**14.1** Trouble with telesales	business problems	group simulation	memo; using capital letters	50 mins
Intermediate	**14.2** What do you do?	describing and managing work	paired text analysis, guessing game	job description	50 mins
Upper-intermediate	**14.3** Mr Don't Know	recruiting people	paired text analysis	employment reference; emphasising ambiguity	50 mins
15 Money					
Elementary	**15.1** Credit cards	borrowing money	paired simulation	form, semi-formal letter (request)	50 mins
Intermediate	**15.2** Shopping by post	returning faulty goods	paired text analysis	form, semi-formal letter (complaint); error correction	50 mins
Upper-intermediate	**15.3** Can't pay; won't pay!	delaying payment	paired simulation	formal letter (responding to demands, making excuses)	50 mins
16 Past experiences and stories					
Elementary	**16.1** One thing led to another …	planning stories	group game	fiction; plotting a story	50 mins
Intermediate	**16.2** The six friends	inventing fictional answers	group role play	personal letter (explanatory); varying viewpoint	50 mins
Upper-intermediate	**16.3** The storyteller	memorable events retold	group storytelling	fiction; drafting	50 mins
17 Science and technology					
Elementary	**17.1** Short circuits	simple electrical circuits	paired game	sequenced description	50 mins
Intermediate	**17.2** It's amazing …	selling new inventions	pair simulation	catalogue description	50 mins
Upper-intermediate	**17.3** www. worldwideweb?	access to the Internet	interpreting data	comparative report; describing changes and trends	50 mins
18 Social and environmental issues					
Elementary	**18.1** Planning problems	a new bypass	group simulation	petition; expanding ideas	50 mins
Intermediate	**18.2** Campaign, not complain	campaigning	paired simulation	semi-formal letter (protest)	50 mins
Upper-intermediate	**18.3** Water: a clear solution	clean water, development	paired simulation	e-mail campaigning; presenting opinion	50 mins

Introduction

Who is *Writing Extra* for?

Writing Extra is a resource book containing photocopiable materials for supplementary classroom work. The activities provide self-contained lessons for the busy teacher. Each activity consists of a page of clear, step-by-step instructions for the teacher and a photocopiable page for the students. The material is aimed at young adults (16+) and adult learners; however, most activities can be easily adapted for the needs of younger students. *Writing Extra* offers teachers an exciting collection of topic-based skills activities from elementary to upper-intermediate level.

How will *Writing Extra* help my students?

Writing Extra is designed to make your students *want* to write. It motivates them through a variety of activities such as role play, puzzle-solving and text analysis, which enable students to practise all four skills while focusing on a definite written outcome. By providing meaningful contexts which lead to practical writing tasks such as e-mail, letters, reports and diaries, it encourages students to develop an awareness of both the reader and the specific form being practised.

How is *Writing Extra* organised?

Writing Extra is divided into 18 units, each focusing on a different theme. Each unit approaches the theme from an interesting and original angle. The themes cover many of the popular topics found in standard coursebooks. Therefore the activities can be used to supplement existing course material, offering diversity and a refreshing approach to these familiar themes. Each unit offers three activities at the following levels: elementary, intermediate and upper-intermediate. A map of the book provides a clear overview of the 54 activities, enabling the teacher to quickly locate a suitable activity for their class. A Writing tool kit at the end of the book includes reference sheets for students on style and organisation.

How is each activity organised?

Each activity has one page of step-by-step teacher's notes and a photocopiable sheet on the opposite page for the students.

There is minimal preparation before class. Usually teachers simply have to photocopy and cut up the appropriate number of sheets.

The teacher's notes include a key information panel for quick reference. The headings in this section are:

Level	elementary, intermediate or upper-intermediate
Topic	a brief description of the topic, e.g. *Identifying famous people*
Activity type	a brief description of the activity students will be doing, whether they are working in pairs, groups, etc.
Writing focus	the particular form of writing that is practised
Time	suggested timing for the Warm up and Main activity. These are only guidelines and timing may vary from class to class
Key language	vocabulary and structures that your students will encounter during the activity
Preparation	what needs to be done before the lesson, ie. how many copies of the photocopiable sheet you need to make, what cutting is required, or whether you need to bring anything else to the lesson

The lesson is divided into these three stages:

Warm up	– provides the context and some vocabulary for the task
Main activity	– sets the task and generally presents a model or template
	– students produce the first draft, which they sometimes correct using a checklist
Follow up	– students can do further optional practice or practise a connected form, either in class, if there's time, or for homework

What is the best way to use *Writing Extra* in the classroom?

Each *Writing Extra* activity focuses on a practical task which explores the style and content of a particular form and thus encourages students to concentrate on communicating effectively. Many activities employ paired or group writing to enable students to develop their own pieces in a supportive atmosphere. By pairing an imaginative student with a more linguistically confident classmate, the teacher can enable both to produce a better piece of writing than either could produce on their own. Encouraging students to draft initially on alternate lines also enables them to refine their piece later on without rewriting the whole thing. By promoting such focused drafting, redrafting and self-evaluation, using the material in the Writing tool kit at the back of the book, the teacher can encourage students to take control of their own learning.

Through realistic real-world content and a mix of light and serious topics, *Writing Extra* encourages students to draw on their existing knowledge and skills in their written pieces: supported by models and templates, they produce realistic written texts through a process of informed criticism. This releases the classroom teacher to become audience and assistant, constantly monitoring and offering support and advice. Once the piece is finished the teacher can join with the student, who may well become their own best critic, in evaluating the piece! The Writing tool kit includes checklists, correction codes and an evaluation scale to further this end. It also includes photocopiable students' reference sheets on organisation and style, some suggestions on potential resources such as the Internet and further tips on using the book.

This book is part of a family of skills books in the Cambridge Copy Collection series. The other books available are *Listening Extra, Speaking Extra* and *Reading Extra,* and they each follow a similar format.

Thanks and acknowledgements

This book is dedicated to James and Izzy for playtime, hugs and wonder.

The author would like to thank the following:

Bernard Gilhooly, John Singleton and Geoff Sutton for teaching me not to be precious about my own writing; Derek Spafford, Kevin Higgins, Simon Barnes, Rebecca Rowntree, Alan Wilson and Beverley Sedley for giving me the space to learn the ABC of EFL; Michael Black, Rick Baldwin and Vicki Hollett for support early on; Chris George and Fiona McCartney for use of the Bell School (Cambridge) Study Centre; Nóirín Burke, Martine Walsh and Sarah Almy for their vision and tireless work on *Writing Extra*; and last, but very far from least, Katy for insanely sticking by me, pizza and two wonderful children.

The author and publishers would like to thank the following individuals for their help in commenting on the material, piloting it with their students and providing invaluable feedback:

Sharon Birbeck, Cambridge, UK

Jana Čadová, Prague, Czech Republic

Jessica Chen, Taiwan

Ludmila Gorodetskaya, Moscow, Russia

Duncan Hindmarch, Stoke-on-Trent, UK

John Irving, Ipswich, UK

Elaine Redford, Clermond-Ferrand, France

Wayne Trotman, Izmir, Turkey

Olga Vinogradova, Moscow, Russia

Alison Michelle Wain, Cairo, Egypt

Gillian West, Muscat, Oman

The author and publishers are grateful to the authors, publishers and others who have given permission for the use of copyright material identified in the text. It has not been possible to identify the sources of all the material used and in such cases the publishers would welcome information from copyright owners.

p.37 Cambridge Newspapers Ltd; p.51 Fairtrade; p.57 The Women's Press / Joan Barfoot; p.61 Cambridge International Dictionary of English, Cambridge University Press, 1995; p.67 *tvchoice*.

Illustrations: Asa Anderson (p.101); Lisa Atkinson (pp.51, 67); Phil Burrows (pp.47, 71); Terry Finnegan (pp.41, 49); Tony Forbes (pp.23, 33); Hardlines (pp.17, 25, 27, 29, 35, 53, 61, 63, 73, 77, 79, 81, 85, 106, 107, 111, 113, 117); Mark MacLaughlin (pp.31, 41); Martin Smith (pp.15, 57, 109); Sam Thompson (pp.43, 53, 101); Jonathan Williams (pp.17, 87).

Text design: Hardlines, Park St, Charlbury, Oxford

Page make-up: Hardlines, Park St, Charlbury, Oxford

Cover illustration: Tim Kahane

Cover design: Hardlines, Park St, Charlbury, Oxford

1.1

Pickpocket!

LEVEL
Elementary

TOPIC
Identifying people,
crime

ACTIVITY TYPE
Group role play

**WRITING
FOCUS**
Form, statement

TIME
50 minutes

KEY LANGUAGE
course, interests and
hobbies, membership,
nationality, occupation,
pickpocket, receipt,
title, victim;

Wh- questions

PREPARATION
One photocopy of
Contents of Wallet, cut
up, for each group of
four students; one
photocopy of the Police
Form for each student;
for Follow up, one
photocopy of the Police
Form for each student

Optionally, one
simplified photocopy of
the Second draft
checklist (p.120) for
each student

Warm up

1 Ask a student to walk across the classroom. Mime taking their wallet from their pocket. Ask: *What did I do?* Elicit the noun *pickpocket* and the phrasal verb *to pick somebody's pocket*.

2 Ask: *Has anyone ever had something stolen from their pocket? What was it? How did they get it back?*

Main activity

1 Tell the students they are police officers who have found a stolen wallet in London's Oxford Street. The wallet does not contain an address, or any money or credit cards; they will need to find out as much as possible about its owner if they are to return it. Elicit what documents might be in the wallet and what information they might contain.

2 Divide the class into groups of four and give each group one set of the Contents of Wallet. Tell the students to discuss what the documents are and what they tell them about the wallet's owner. Feedback as a whole class.

3 Give out one copy of the Police Form per student and ask them to complete the form. They should write full sentences under the heading Interests and hobbies.

4 Feedback as a whole class. Elicit the correct question for each piece of information and write the question on the left of the board and the answer on the right:

What's his surname?	*Parker*
What's his first name?	*Peter*
Mr, Mrs, Miss or Ms?	*Mr*
When was he born?	*21 May 1984*
Where does he live?	*We don't know.*
What's his telephone number?	*We don't know.*
What does he do?	*Student*
Where does he come from?	*We don't know.*
What are his interests and hobbies?	*He is studying English Literature and enjoys music. He likes travelling (he has an International Student Travel Card), keeping fit, swimming and/or playing squash.*

5 Explain that Peter has gone to the police station. Write these cues on the board: *My name is … / When I was … / … was stolen / It had lots of important things in it like …* In pairs, tell students to write Peter's statement to the police, using the cues to help them.

6 Tell the students to swap their statement with another pair and check the language. You may want to give students a simplified Second draft checklist to help them with this (see p.120).

7 Display the finished statements on the wall with one set of the Contents of Wallet. In groups of three or four, tell the students to select the statement which is most factually accurate.

Follow up

- Ask the students how much information about themselves they think is in their own wallet. Give each student a second copy of the Police Form and ask them to use their own wallet to complete it. Tell them not to add any information that is not included in the wallet.

- Ask the students to complete the story: *'Yesterday, Peter Parker went shopping …'.*

Contents of Wallet

Brent Valley University Library Card

Student Name:	Peter Parker
Course:	BA (Hons) English Literature

South Ealing Sports & Fitness Centre

Membership card
No.**567823**

Expires: **August 2004**

This card must be used when
booking squash courts or time in the

Shepherds Bush Empire

COSMIC CHICKEN + SUPPORT BAND

Doors open: 8.00 p.m.
30 March 2004

£15.00   Seat: A32

International Student Travel Card

Name: Parker, Peter
Brent Valley University
DoB: 21/05/1984

N. Patel
Newsagent
Ealing

28.03.04

BBC Music Magazine   £3.99

£3.99

Thank you for
shopping with us

Police Form

Metropolitan Police	Details of Victim		Crime Report Form
Surname:	**First name:**		
Title: Mr/Mrs/Miss/Ms	**Date of birth:**		
Address:	**Telephone number:**		
Occupation:	**Nationality:**		
Interests and hobbies:			

1.2

LEVEL
Intermediate

TOPIC
Identifying famous
people

ACTIVITY TYPE
Paired puzzle-solving,
text analysis

**WRITING
FOCUS**
Biography

TIME
50 minutes

KEY LANGUAGE
*to break a record,
education, major
achievement, scorer,
to sign a contract,
success, transferred,
to turn something
down;*
Question forms

PREPARATION
One photocopy for
each pair of students; a
list of ten famous
people that your
students
will know

Optionally, one
simplified photocopy
of the First draft
checklist (p.120) for
each student

Note: You may want to
download more
examples of
biographies from
www.biography.com

Who's who

Warm up

1 Divide the class into groups of four. Write a famous person's name on the board. Ask the groups to discuss everything they know about that person.

2 After two minutes, feedback onto the board as a whole class. Use these headings: *Name; Occupation; Achievements; When/where they were born; What their education was; What jobs they have done.*

Main activity

1 Put the students in pairs and give each pair a photocopy of the Sample Biographies. Ask them to read them and guess the names of the people. Feedback as a whole class.

> **Answer key**
> **A** Ronaldo (Luis Nazá de Lima)   **B** J.K. Rowling

2 Tell the students to use the Warm up headings to identify where different information is given in the Sample Biographies. Feedback as a whole class and emphasise the level of formality of the language.

3 Explain that they are going to gather information on another student, so that they can write a brief biography. Students who do not have much lifetime experience may wish to do this in 'role' by thinking of a famous person or selecting one from the list the teacher prepared before the lesson. Tell them not to tell anyone who they are!

4 Divide the class into groups of four and ask them to brainstorm the sort of questions they are going to have to ask. Feedback as a whole class. Write these cues on the board as students feedback: *Was born in … (place?) / Was educated … / Worked as … / Major achievement … / Free-time achievement … .*

5 Put the students in pairs and ask them to interview their partners and make notes, using the cues on the board to help them.

6 When students have had sufficient time, stop them and ask them to write their partner's biography. Tell them to ensure they do not write a name on the biography.

7 Ask them to swap their written biographies with their partner and tell them to check them for factual content and organisation and redraft the biographies together. You may want to give students a simplified First draft checklist to help with this (see p.120).

8 Display the finished biographies around the classroom and ask the students to read them and try to identify who is who!

Follow up

- Ask the students to write the biography of a fictional character, e.g. Sherlock Holmes, Hamlet or Cinderella.

- Ask the students to rewrite their own biography for the first page of their website. Emphasise how this may differ, e.g. it will probably use less formal language and might focus on achievements and hobbies rather than education and career. It will also be written in the first person.

Sample Biographies

A

................?................. (1976 -), footballer. He was born in Rio de Janeiro, Brazil. By the age of 16 he was already playing in the Brazilian First Division and scored 54 goals in 54 games. Two years later, he became a member of Brazil's World Cup team and joined PSV Eindhoven to become Holland's top scorer for that season. In 1996 he transferred for a record $19.2 million to the Spanish club FC Barcelona, who went on to win the European Cup Winner's Cup. In the same year he won a bronze medal with the Brazilian team at the Olympics. In the late 1990s he was voted European Player of the Year and twice International Footballer of the Year. 1997 saw him sign to the Italian club Inter Milan and win the Copa America. He joined Brazil's World Cup team in 1998 and, after recovering from several injuries, scored two decisive goals in the 2002 finals against Germany. In the same year he signed to Spanish club Real Madrid.
................?................. is widely believed to be Brazil's best player since Pele.

B

................?................. (1965 -), writer of children's books. Born in Chipping Sodbury, England, she was educated at Wyedean Comprehensive School and Exeter University before becoming a teacher of French and English. In 1990 she began writing the first of a planned series of seven books about her famous wizard and his stay at Hogwarts School of Witchcraft and Wizardry. The first book was turned down by several companies before finally appearing in 1997, when it was an instant success. Her following books broke many publishing records. By 2000, ...?................. was the world's highest earning author and within two years her books had sold over 167 million copies worldwide. The film versions followed and the fifth book in the series was published in 2003.
................?................. was recognised for services to Britain in 2000 with the award of an OBE (Order of the British Empire).

1.3

Jobsearch

LEVEL
Upper-intermediate

TOPIC
Jobs

ACTIVITY TYPE
Group game, role
play, text analysis

**WRITING
FOCUS**
CV (Curriculum Vitae)

TIME
50 minutes

KEY LANGUAGE
*initiating, liaising, to
nurture, ongoing,
programme, stock*;

Past tenses; omission
of subject pronouns

PREPARATION
One set of Pictures, cut
up, for each group of
four students; one
photocopy of Previous
Employment Details for
each pair of students

Optionally, one
photocopy of the First
draft checklist (p.120)
for each student

Note: You may want to
download examples of
CVs from
www.jobstar.org/tools
/resume

Warm up

1   In groups of four, give each group a set of Pictures. Ask each student to take one picture. Explain that they are going to create information about that person. Ask them to write on the picture a fictional name and age for the person. Give them five minutes to use their imagination and write on a separate piece of paper brief notes about the person, e.g. job, family, qualifications, etc.

2   Ask the students to swap their picture with someone else in the group. Tell them not to talk together. Ask them to write on the back of the new picture what job they think that person might have done in their earlier life and what their hobbies are.

3   Tell the students to swap back their pictures. Ask them to tell the group about their character, using the person's previous job and hobbies, as well as their own notes. The group should try to provide logical reasons for any inconsistencies in their career.

Main activity

1   Write *CV* on the board. Brainstorm what a curriculum vitae is, i.e. a short summary of your career and experiences which you send to a company when you are looking for a job. Elicit why conciseness is important, i.e. because employers receive many CVs and have limited time: if your CV is too long it will not even be read!

2   Elicit what is normally included and, as students feedback, write these headings on the board: *Name; Address; Qualifications; Details of present employment and responsibilities; Details of previous employment and responsibilities; Hobbies; Referees.* Elicit how the information given under *Name, Address, Qualifications, Hobbies* and *Referees* will be factual and in list form, while the information on current and previous employment will be subjective and presented in complete paragraphs.

3   Give each group two copies of the Previous Employment Details. In pairs, ask them to read the details and do the vocabulary exercise. Feedback as a whole class.

> **Answer key**
> **1** initiating   **2** developing   **3** liaising   **4** nurtured   **5** delighted   **6** ongoing

Elicit why the writer has used a formal style, i.e. because CVs are written for a business context, and how it 'sells' the person to the company by presenting everything in a positive way.

4   Brainstorm the characteristics of the layout, i.e. dates; job; company/employer; location; responsibilities and description of the person's contribution to the company; and the style, i.e. formal, concise, subject omitted in the first sentence. **Note:** The person in this example works for the local government, Hertfordshire County Council.

5   Ask the students to decide on a job their fictional character from the Warm up would like to apply for. Ask them to write the character's CV, using the headings from step 2.

6   After ten minutes, ask them to swap CVs with another student. Tell them to check the new CV for organisation and style and correct it. You may want to give students a copy of the First draft checklist to help them with this (see p.120).

7   Ask the students to swap back CVs and in their pairs discuss/agree any corrections.

Follow up

● Tell students to find a job advertisement that interests them in a newspaper and write their own CV in English, targeted at that particular job.

● Tell the students they have seen a job advertisement which interests them, and need to write a formal letter to enclose with their CV when applying for the job. It must include: where they saw the advertisement; a brief summary of why they want the job and why they would be good at it.

Pictures

Name:	Name:	Name:	Name:
Age:	Age:	Age:	Age:

Previous Employment Details

1999 – 2003

Chief Librarian, Stevenage Library (Hertfordshire County Council)

Responsible for managing a team of ten people, initiating a staff training programme on the Internet and developing the stock to include more popular fiction books. The job also involved liaising with many outside companies in order to raise money for additional books and computers. During my time as Chief Librarian I nurtured a strong team spirit and was delighted when the library service asked me to share this experience with colleagues around the country as part of their ongoing training programme.

Find formal words in the text that mean the same as these words:

1 starting   **2** expanding   **3** working with   **4** encouraged   **5** extremely pleased   **6** continuing

2.1

Dinner's in the oven

LEVEL
Elementary

TOPIC
Relationships, food

ACTIVITY TYPE
Paired matching,
text analysis

**WRITING
FOCUS**
Personal note

TIME
50 minutes

KEY LANGUAGE
Vocabulary of food
and household items;
*economy (adj.),
hands off, to be out
of something,
shared house, vet*;

Omission of articles,
auxilary verbs and
pronouns

PREPARATION
One photocopy, cut up,
for each pair of students

Warm up

1 Write on the board in the style of a brief note: *Gone to see Mum. Back for dinner. Steve*

2 Write on the board: *Who wrote this note? Why? Where are they? How old do you think they are? Who do you think they live with?* In pairs, ask the students to answer the questions. Feedback as a whole class. Do not confirm or reject any ideas.

3 Ask: *Who writes notes in your house? Who are the notes to? What are they about?*

Main activity

1 Keep the students in pairs, and give each pair a set of Notes. Explain they are from three different households. Ask them to try to answer the questions on the board for each note. Feedback as a whole class. Do not confirm or reject any ideas.

2 Give the students the Shopping and Household cards. Explain they must match a note and three items of shopping to each household. Feedback as a whole class. At this stage, ask students to justify their answers.

> **Suggested answer**
> **Note A:** Household 3; dog food, aftershave, croissant
> **Note B:** Household 1; chocolates, nappies, fresh salmon
> **Note C:** Household 2; chips, white sliced bread, burgers

3 Ask the students to expand the notes into complete sentences.

> **Answer key**
> **Note A: I have** taken Ben to the vet. **Our/Your** dinner **is** in the oven.
> **Note B: We are** out of milk. Can you get some on the way back from work? **I** love you. **P/Philip**
> **Note C:** Sue **keep your** hands off my food!

Brainstorm what was omitted in the notes, i.e. subject pronouns and auxiliary verbs.

4 Ask the students to each write a typical note for their own or a friend's household, in the same style as the notes they have seen. They must not use their real name!

5 In the same pairs, ask the students to swap notes and answer these two questions: *Do I understand the message? What does this note tell me about the household?* Explain that one student in each pair is Student A and the other Student B. Tell them to discuss if the notes reveal enough about their household and then redraft the notes, with Student A acting as secretary and writing out both notes.

6 Ask each pair to think of three items of shopping for each of their households. Tell them to ensure the shopping reveals enough about their two households. Student A should then write out the two shopping lists, one for each household.

7 Ask the students to write a description of their own household. Ask them to check them for accuracy and then ask Student B to act as secretary and write out the two descriptions.

8 Join the pairs into groups of four. Ask each group to swap its Notes, Lists and Households with another group. Tell the groups to match the new Notes and Lists to the Households and check their answers with the group they have swapped with.

Follow up

- Ask the students to write a typical note and shopping list for a famous person. Ask the other students to guess the famous person.

- Ask the students to write the note that they would most like to receive from a member of their family.

Notes

A

Taken Ben to the vet. Dinner's in the oven.

B

Out of milk. Can you get some on way back from work? Love you. P

C

SUE, HANDS OFF MY FOOD!

Shopping

Dog food

Aftershave

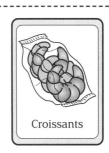
Croissants

Chips

Burgers

Belgian chocolates

Salmon

Nappies

White sliced bread

Households

Household 1: Philip is a computer consultant and Sue works in a shop. They have a ten-month-old baby boy, Ben.

Household 2: Peter is a university student who lives in a shared house.

Household 3: Sue and Tim have been married for 15 years and have a small dog called Ben. Sue is a bank manager and Tim is a teacher.

2.2

LEVEL
Intermediate

TOPIC
Marriage

ACTIVITY TYPE
Group role play

WRITING FOCUS
Personal letter (apology)

TIME
50 minutes

KEY LANGUAGE
to achieve something, a bad influence, to be desperate for (something), inherit, in-laws, to settle down;
Language of apology, explaining feelings

PREPARATION
One photocopy, cut up, of the Role Cards for each group of four students; one photocopy of the Letter Cues for each pair of students

Trouble with the in-laws

Warm up

1   Draw these family trees on the board and elicit the relationships between the people.

Philip	┬	Mary		John	┬	Kath
	Mark (23)				Tina (33)	

2   Ask: *What will the relationships be if Mark and Tina get married?* Elicit the vocabulary *in-laws*. Ask: *Do you think the age difference could be a problem?*

Main activity

1   Explain that Mark and Tina have asked both sets of parents for a meal at Mark's flat. At the meal Mark and Tina announce that they are getting married. Their parents are very upset.

2   Divide the class into four equal groups, and explain that each group represents one of the parents. If the class does not divide into equal groups, ensure that three of the groups are equal and the fourth smaller. Give each student the appropriate Role Card, ensuring that the smallest group get the role of Kath. Tell them to discuss in their groups what they think of the announcement and how they will react to it.

3   Regroup the students into new groups of four so that all the parents are represented in each group. If the group numbers are unequal, the role of Kath will be omitted from some groups. Tell them Mark and Tina have left the room to get coffee and this is their first opportunity to talk about the marriage. They should say what is on their minds and defend themselves and their son/daughter against any insult!

4   After five minutes, interrupt the discussion. Tell them that they are so upset with what's been said that they leave the dinner party early. Mark and Tina have also overheard everything and are in tears.

5   Explain that the parents feel terrible about what has happened and are going to write letters apologising to Mark and Tina and to the other parents. Elicit how these letters will differ and what they will include, e.g. the letter to Mark and Tina will be less formal than the one to the other parents, but both will include an apology, an explanation of their viewpoint and also how they want to move matters forward.

6   Give each pair of parents a copy of the Letter Cues and ask one of the students to write to Mark and Tina and the other to write to the other parents, using the cues to help them. If the role of Kath has been omitted from any groups, put the spare Johns in pairs to write the letters.

7   After ten to fifteen minutes stop them and ask them to swap their letters with their partner and check them for logic and persuasiveness. Ask the students to feedback to each other and redraft their letters.

Follow up

●   Ask the students to swap their letters with students who were in role as the other parents. Ask them to read the new letter, decide how persuasive it is and write a reply, either accepting or rejecting the apology.

●   Explain that Mark and Tina got married and Tina is now pregnant. She wants to develop her career and they plan that Mark will give up his job to look after the baby. Tell the students to write Mark and Tina's letter to their parents explaining their plans.

Role Cards

Philip (Group 1)

You are Mark's father. You think he is much too young to settle down. He cannot possibly know for certain that he wants to spend the rest of his life with Tina. Besides, her family have no money and Mark will inherit the family business.

Mary (Group 2)

You are Mark's mother. He is your 'little boy' and still needs someone to take care of him. Since he started going out with Tina you have been very worried. You think she is a bad influence on him and far too old.

John (Group 3)

You are Tina's father. You are proud of what Tina has achieved. It is not everyone who gets to be a senior manager at the age of 33. Mark has not even got a good job! And if they have children, he will expect her to give up her job to look after them.

Kath (Group 4)

You are Tina's mother. You are desperate for some grandchildren. You are not happy about Mark though. He is too young. While Tina is seeing him, she is not getting to meet men her own age.

Letter Cues

Letter 1: Dear Tina and Mark	**Letter 2: Dear Mr and Mrs ....**
Paragraph 1: Apologising	*Paragraph 1: Apologising*
We're so sorry for …	We're writing to apologise for …
We're really/awfully sorry for …	Please accept our apologies for …
How silly of us to say that …	Please forgive us for saying …
… We really didn't mean it.	… it was a misunderstanding.
We were amazed at …	… came as a great surprise.
Paragraph 2: Explaining	*Paragraph 2: Explaining*
We're very happy/unhappy about …	We were shocked/surprised to hear that …
We think …	As we see it …
You see …	In our opinion …
Paragraph 3: Making plans	*Paragraph 3: Making plans*
We hope we can …	We would be really pleased if we could …
Let's hope we can …	We would like to think we can …
Lots of love	Yours sincerely
Mum and Dad	Mr and Mrs ....

2.3

Family matters ...

LEVEL
Upper-intermediate

TOPIC
Genealogy

ACTIVITY TYPE
Simulation

WRITING FOCUS
E-mail, register

TIME
50 minutes

KEY LANGUAGE
archives, attachment, database, distantly related, genealogy, originated from, siblings, typifies

PREPARATION
One photocopy, cut up, for each student; one photocopy of the First draft checklist (p.120) for each student

Warm up

1 Write on the board: *genealogy*. Brainstorm what it is and how you could find out about your family's history, e.g. by asking relatives, using archives or the Internet.

2 Give each student a copy of the E-mail. Explain they received it this morning from someone who they do not know. Ask them to read it quickly and discuss with a partner what the person wants them to do. Feedback as a whole class.

Main activity

1 Elicit how the e-mail is in a semi-formal style since the writer does not know the recipient but is sending a personal and not a business e-mail.

2 Write this table on the board:

> 1 a. *I have contacted my brother concerning this.* / b. *I've got in touch with my brother about it.*
>
> 2 a. *Yeah, I'll do it!* / b. *I would be very interested in doing it.*
>
> 3 a. *Many thanks for your e-mail.* / b. *Cheers for the message.*
>
> 4 a. *It was good to hear from you.* / b. *I appreciate you contacting me.*

In the same pairs, ask the students to quickly choose the phrases in the table which are most likely to appear in their reply and decide the order in which they would appear.

Answer key
3 a   **2** b   **1** a   **4** b

Elicit how these are all semi-formal and therefore appropriate in a reply to a stranger.

3 Ask the students individually to write a positive reply to the e-mail. In it they should agree to contribute to the website at a later date but not yet give any information.

4 After five minutes, ask the students to swap their e-mail with the other student in their pair and check the new e-mail for the level of formality. Ask them to underline anything they feel is too informal and return it for redrafting.

5 Give each student a copy of the E-mail Attachment and elicit what it is, i.e. separate information that has been attached to the main e-mail. Ask the students to read it and discuss in their pairs who will have access to the information and how much about themselves they wish to share. Feedback as a whole class.

6 Ask the students individually to write their text for the database. If they feel uncomfortable writing about their own family, tell them to write about an imaginary family.

7 After fifteen minutes, ask the students to swap their text with their partner. Give each student a copy of the First draft checklist. Ask them to read their partner's text and underline any problems of communication, style or organisation.

8 Ask the students to return the annotated text to their partner, discuss any annotations with them and then redraft their own text.

9 If there is enough time, put the students in groups of four. Tell them to fold over the top of their texts so that you cannot see the first section entitled 'Me'. Ask them to swap their texts with another group, discuss the new ones and guess who they refer to. They can then check by unfolding them.

Follow up

● Ask the students to write a semi-formal e-mail declining to submit information for the database and explaining their reasons.

● Ask the students to rewrite the information in the attachment for a 'Family Book' that will be distributed only to close family members. They should choose an appropriate style and may choose to add or omit things.

E-mail

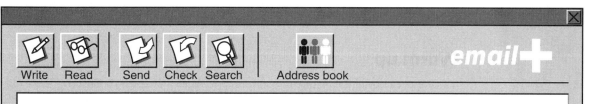

Write Read   Send Check Search   Address book

I hope you do not mind me contacting you. I obtained your details from an Internet e-mail directory and am e-mailing everyone who shares the same family name in your locality. My grandparents originated from there and I believe we may be distantly related.

In order to aid my research, and that of others, I am attempting to establish a genealogical database on my family website. I was hoping you might consider contributing some information about yourself and your immediate family. I would be grateful if you could forward this message to any other family members who you feel might be interested.

I do hope you will give this serious consideration. I have attached some notes if you would like to take this further. Many thanks for your help.

Best regards

Click for
Attachment

E-mail Attachment

The Family History Database

This searchable database will appear on my website. As well as names and dates, I would like it to include some more interesting information about the family that you feel comfortable about sharing with others.

To help you I have split the information into three sections:
Me; My family; What makes my family special or different.

Please limit yourself to a maximum of 200 words per section.

Me
Information about who you are, where you were born and what you do.

My family
Brief biographical information on your siblings, parents and grandparents.

What makes my family special or different
Memories of your childhood home; any incident that has made your life slightly different to others' in the family; any incident or event that you can think of that typifies being part of the family.

3.1

Nothing happened today

LEVEL
Elementary

TOPIC:
Routines, relationships

ACTIVITY TYPE
Paired text analysis

WRITING FOCUS
Diary entry, memoir

TIME
50 minutes

KEY LANGUAGE
band, college, entry, live music, memoirs, to waste time;

Omission of articles, auxiliary verbs and pronouns; adverbs of frequency; past simple

PREPARATION
One photocopy, cut up, for each student

Warm up

1   Give one copy of the picture to each student. As a whole class, brainstorm: *How old is she? Where is she? What does she do? What do you think she did yesterday?*

2   Give one copy of the Diary Entry to each student. Explain it's an entry from the young woman's diary. Ask them to read the entry to check their guesses. As a whole class, feedback and check difficult vocabulary.

Main activity

1   Explain that it is twenty years later and the woman is now a successful politician. She has decided to publish her memoirs. Give one copy of the Memoir to each student. Tell the students to use the information from the Diary Entry to complete the Memoir about her time at college. Feedback as a whole class.

> **Answer key**
> **1** headache   **2** library   **3** college

2   Discuss how the Diary Entry and Memoir are different, i.e. the diary is not written in complete sentences and uses a variety of tenses; the memoir nearly always uses past tenses. In the diary, routine activities like getting up have been omitted and only interesting and unusual events are included.

3   Copy the diary entry for 23.57 onto the board and mark it to show where words are omitted:

> *Whole evening wasted. MoCo brilliant ... played all their hit songs. Lead singer is*
> ^   ^   ^   ^   ^
> *so good-looking. M spent whole time with Tina.*
>   ^

In pairs, ask the students to add the missing words to make good English sentences.

> **Answer key**
> **The** whole evening **was** wasted. MoCo **were** brilliant ... **they** played all their hit songs. **The** lead singer is so good-looking. **Mark** spent **the** whole time with Tina.

4   As a whole class, brainstorm what types of words have been omitted, i.e. articles, verbs, pronouns. Ask: *Why are diary entries shortened like this?* Explain that it is quicker to write like that, especially when you're putting down a lot of exciting things, and you do not expect other people to read your diary so you can shorten things and not cause any misunderstandings. Note that Mark's name has been abbreviated. This stops anybody who does read the diary knowing who you are talking about!

5   Tell the students to choose one day from last week and write their diary entry for that day. Tell them to make it very interesting and invent details if necessary.

6   After ten minutes, collect in the diaries and redistribute them, making sure each student has a different one. Ask them to read them quickly and guess who wrote them.

Follow up

●   Tell the students to choose the best day or most exciting day in their life and write their diary entry. Alternatively, they could write the entry in the role of a famous person.

●   Ask the students to interview their parents or an older person and write their memoirs. Tell them to use the photocopied memoir as a model, making sure to change it to the third person, and start: *'Twenty years ago ...'*.

Diary Entry

Friday 15 May

13.15: Terrible headache. Must have more sleep! (Not till tomorrow. Got tickets for MoCo at college tonight.) Library full of people not reading books. Am I on the right course? Am going to be a bus driver (won't need exams). Mark didn't even say hello when I walked past. Why are men idiots?! Tina's right: she says I should forget him. Impossible when he's everywhere!

19.08: Should I dress to please M? Really don't know. Yes. Am going to wear my blue t-shirt and black mini. M loves them.

23.57: Whole evening wasted. MoCo brilliant... played all their hit songs. Lead singer is so good-looking. M spent whole time with Tina.

Memoir

Twenty years ago, when I was a student I usually got up at 9.00 and had some toast for breakfast. I nearly always stayed up late, so I often had a bad [1] .... when I first got up! After breakfast, I normally went to the [2] .... Everyone studied hard but I wasn't really interested in all that hard work. I saw all the good bands who played at 3 .... In fact, I still love live music.

3.2

Prison: doing time

LEVEL
Intermediate

TOPIC
Prison routines

ACTIVITY TYPE
Paired text analysis

WRITING FOCUS
Writing a report; editing for length

TIME
50 minutes

KEY LANGUAGE
to be impressed, bedding, to behave, cell, a couple of, lock-up, prison officer, recreation, yard, workshops

PREPARATION
One photocopy, cut up, each pair of students

Optionally, one photocopy of Writing style 1 (p.125) for each student

Warm up

1 Put the students into groups of four. Give each group two copies of the Prison Routines, and ask them to look at the timetable headed Our Group's Prison Day. Explain that they are all chief prison officers in a problem prison. The prisoners are currently locked up in their cells all day, and are bored and becoming aggressive. Their job is to plan a new prison routine for the prisoners. Ask the students to look at the list of Possible Options, and discuss any difficult vocabulary.

2 Give the groups five minutes to plan a new routine. Each numbered slot in the timetable can have one or more options; they can choose from the options provided, and add new options of their own if they wish. They do not have to use all the options and can use the same option more than once. The times for meals and night-time lock-up cannot change.

3 Feedback as a whole class, and ask students to justify the options they chose.

Main activity

1 Give each group two copies of the Letter Extract. Explain that it is part of a letter that Hull Prison's new Chief Prison Officer has written to his friend describing his first day at work. Ask the students to read it and complete the gaps in the Hull Prison Day.

> **Answer key**
> **1** Work   **2** Exercise   **3** Work   **4** Life skills   **5** Recreation

Feedback as whole class and briefly discuss the differences between the students' planned routines and that of Hull Prison.

2 Explain that the Chief Prison Officer has decided to edit his letter to make it shorter and more factual. In pairs, give the students five minutes to cut as much as possible. Tell them to only add words if they are necessary to make the meaning clearer.

> **Suggested answer**
> At quarter to eight, the prisoners were moved to work areas. Before lunch, thirty of the prisoners exercised in the yard. After lunch they returned to work but were tired. Later, five students attended a Life skills class. In the evening two prisoners played pool and others watched TV in the recreation room .

3 Explain that the Chief Prison Officer has been asked by the government to write a factual report on how Hull Prison works. A section of the report is about routine: what prisoners can do, what they have to do and what they are not allowed to do at different times. Brainstorm how it will differ in style from the letter, i.e. it will be formal, precise and use the present simple and modals such as *can* and *may* to emphasise routine and possibility and *must* and *cannot* to emphasise compulsion and prohibition.

4 In pairs, give the students ten minutes to write the section on the prison's routine. Explain they should use exact times and explain the options available to prisoners throughout the day, e.g. in recreation time they can play pool, watch TV or read books.

5 Tell the pairs to swap their report with another pair and check it for formality and logic. You may want to give students a copy of Writing style 1 to help them with this (see p.125). When they have had enough time, ask the pairs to regroup and feedback to each other before correcting their report.

Follow up

● Ask the students to write a similar section of a report on the routine they created in the Warm up. If their routine is too similar, tell them to write about how the routine should be altered at weekends.

● Ask the students to write a brochure entry for an all-inclusive package holiday. In it they should say what it is possible to do throughout the day on the holiday and when.

Prison Routines

Our Group's Prison Day	
07.00-08.00	Breakfast
08.00-10.00	1 ....
10.00-12.00	2 ....
12.00-13.00	Lunch
13.00-15.00	3 ....
15.00-17.00	4 ....
17.00-18.00	Tea
18.00-21.00	5 ....
21.00	Lock up for the night

Possible Options

Choose the best time for prisoners to do these things and write them on Our Group's Prison Day:

Lock-up: time spent locked in cells

Work: washing clothes or working in the kitchen; working in the workshops making clothes or parts for machines

Recreation: prisoners can use a room with a TV, pool table and books, the computer room or the prison library

Education: classes in arts and crafts, basic maths and English and computing

Life skills: practical sessions on problem solving, anger management and social skills

Exercise: prisoners can exercise in the gym or prison yard

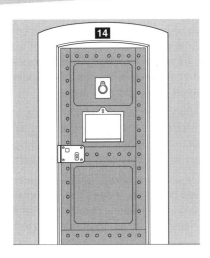

Hull Prison Day	
07.00-08.00	Breakfast
08.00-10.00	1 ....
10.00-12.00	2 ....
12.00-13.00	Lunch
13.00-15.00	3 ....
15.00-17.00	4 ....
17.00-18.00	Tea
18.00-21.00	5 ....
21.00	Lock up for the night

Letter Extract

Everything seems to be working well here. I got to work at about quarter to eight, just as the prisoners were being moved to their work areas by the prison officers. I thought it would be good to show my face in the workshops to let everyone know I'd arrived. In the kitchen, several prisoners were busy cleaning up after breakfast and others in the laundry were doing a good job washing the bedding from last week. I wasn't so impressed in the workshops though. Nobody was working when I walked in but as soon as they saw me they started!

From my office I can see the prison yard. Just before lunch at least thirty of the prisoners were out there kicking a ball about. Later, I went downstairs to see how they behaved on their way back to work. They all seemed pretty tired, which is good.

Late afternoon, I went down to watch a life skills class. There were about five prisoners talking about their experience of street fights. I followed them down to tea, which was well organised. Afterwards, on the way back I passed the recreation room where a couple of prisoners were playing pool and others were watching TV. All in all, I was very pleased with what I saw.

3.3

LEVEL
Upper-intermediate

TOPIC
Crime, alibis

ACTIVITY TYPE
Paired puzzle-solving,
role play

WRITING FOCUS
Summary report,
note taking

TIME
50 minutes

KEY LANGUAGE
affair, to appropriate,
to interrogate,
interrogations,
to investigate, lover,
paperwork, to stab,
suspect, wound;

Modals of deduction
(*could have been,*
might have been, etc)

PREPARATION
One photocopy of the
Summary of
Circumstances for each
pair of students; one
copy of the Role Cards
for each group; one
copy of the First draft
checklist (p.120) for
each pair of students

Murder mystery

Warm up

Explain that there has been a mysterious death. In pairs, give each pair a copy of the Summary of Circumstances and tell them to discuss what could have happened to the man. After five minutes, feedback as a whole class. Do not confirm or deny anything!

Main activity

1   Keep the class as one group. With larger classes, divide the students into equal groups no larger than twelve students. Choose the most imaginative pair and give them each a Role Card. Tell them they knew the murdered man, Ted Naccain. The rest of their group are police officers who will interrogate them about his death in five minutes' time. They must prepare by reading the information on their card; they can add more details if they wish. They should not share any information with each other.

2   Tell the other students they are police officers who are investigating the death, which occurred today. They are going to question two people who knew Ted Naccain well and who are possible suspects. Explain that they must try to find out Ted's normal routine and if it has changed at all over the last two days. In their group(s), tell them to appoint one student to act as interrogator and brainstorm a list of questions for the interrogations.

3   After five minutes, stop the group(s). As a whole class, brainstorm how they will structure their note-taking during the interrogations to help them make sense of what has happened. Elicit the headings: *Ted's routine; Changes in routine; Possible reasons for death.* Elicit how a mind-map may be easier to complete for the first two headings and a list for the third. Elicit how the notes will be brief, incomplete sentences.

4   Tell the two 'suspects' in each group to introduce themselves. Tell the groups that their appointed interrogator has five minutes to interrogate each person, starting with Simon Naccain. The suspects are not allowed to talk to each other. During the interrogation, the other students in the group should take notes so that they can complete a police report.

5   After ten minutes, stop the interrogations and ask the students who have been in role to rejoin the class. Brainstorm how the report will be formal, in the third person and will use modals of deduction to talk about the past, e.g. *may + have +* third form of verb. Quickly brainstorm modals on the board, from impossible on the left to possible on the right, i.e. *can't, might, may, could, must.*

6   In their pairs, ask the students to write the police report using these headings: *Routine and any changes to the routine; Possible reasons for the death.*

7   Give each pair a copy of the First draft checklist. Tell each pair to swap their report with another pair and use the symbols from the checklist to mark any changes they feel need to be made to the style of the report or to make it clearer or more logical.

8   Tell the pairs to swap back their reports and correct them where appropriate.

9   As a whole class, feedback possible solutions to Ted's death.

> **Suggested answer**
> One possible solution: Ted Naccain is an anagram of *an accident*! He was working when a bird flew into the closed window. Ted went to investigate the noise, opened the window, leant out and an icicle fell from the roof and stabbed into his back. He fell backwards and died. The icicle melted, mixing with his blood on the floor.

Follow up

●   Explain that €1,000 went missing from the school office yesterday afternoon and the students are all suspects. In pairs, ask the students to interview their partner about their normal routine and what they were doing yesterday afternoon. Tell them to take notes about their partner and write a police report with these headings: *The suspect's routine and any changes to the routine; Whether the suspect could have committed the crime and when.*

●   Ask the students to write a press release to give to the media concerning Mr Naccain's death. It must be concise and unambiguous. They must decide what information to release and what information to hold back in case it influences a criminal trial.

Summary of Circumstances

Key
1 body
2 blood
3 office chair
4 desk
5 door – locked
6 window – open
7 security camera – not working

It is Wednesday afternoon and Ted Naccain has been found dead in his office on the second floor of a four storey office block. The body was discovered by Ted's brother, Simon, and the company's accountant, Andrea Christie, at 14.27. When they got there the door was locked and the security camera was not working.

Ted's keys are in his pocket. He is lying on his back in a pool of blood and there is a stab wound to his back but no weapon. It is a cold winter's day and the heaters are full on but the office window is open. There are no footprints in the snow under the open window but there is a dead bird on the ground with no obvious injury.

Role Cards

Simon Naccain

You are Ted's brother and business partner. For the last six months, you've been having an affair with his wife, Gerry. He spends afternoons in meetings, right up until eight o'clock in the evening. That's when you get to see her! She phoned early today and said she thought Ted had found out. That would explain the way he was this morning. You go jogging with him at six o'clock every day and then he gives you a lift to work at about seven. This morning he was late and ran like he was crazy.

At the office, he works hard on paperwork and answering e-mails up until ten when he has some coffee. From then till lunch he's never off the phone, setting up meetings. Today, Andrea Christie called you at lunchtime saying something was wrong. Ted never locks his office door, so when he didn't answer you broke it down.

Andrea Christie

You are the company accountant. You have been appropriating part of the company's profit. Somehow Ted found out. Yesterday afternoon, when he dropped into the office, as he always does around five, he said he wanted your resignation and all the money back by midday on Wednesday. If not, he'd tell the police about it.

You normally meet Ted at one o'clock for lunch in the nearby sandwich bar. After lunch you take cheques to his office for Ted to sign. He didn't show up for lunch today. When you found his office door locked, you tried his mobile and heard it ringing inside. So you called his brother and he broke the door down.

4.1

Designer kitchen

LEVEL
Elementary

TOPIC
Kitchens,
good design

ACTIVITY TYPE
Group
problem-solving

**WRITING
FOCUS**
Report

TIME:
50 minutes

KEY LANGUAGE
Kitchen vocabulary
(e.g. *drawer, electric
kettle, fridge, oven,
sink*, etc.); *clients,
to design something,
washing-up,
work surfaces*;

Conjunctions: *but,
because, also, and*;
prepositions of
location; *should*

PREPARATION
One photocopy, cut up,
for each pair of
students
Note: If you have an
OHP, you may want to
put the photocopiable
page on an OHT to use
at step 3

Warm up

Explain to the students that they work for a company that designs kitchens. Some people have asked for help. Their small flat has a tiny, badly designed kitchen and even making a cup of instant coffee is difficult. Brainstorm what they think the design problems might be.

Main activity

1   In pairs, give each pair a copy of the Report:Part 1. Tell them to read it and complete the vocabulary exercise. Feedback as a whole class.

> **Answer key**
> **1** fridge   **2** oven   **3** drawer   **4** sink   **5** electric kettle

Check to see how many problems the students predicted, and that they understand the problems listed in the report.

2   Give out one copy of the cut-up Kitchen Plan to each pair. If you have prepared an OHT of the kitchen plan, use it here. Explain that they must redesign the kitchen so it takes the fewest possible movements to make a cup of coffee. They already have a sink, a fridge and a cooker to place on the plan. They must decide what the three blank squares represent and label them, e.g. *cupboards, drawers*; these too must be arranged on the plan. The students must also write in where they would put the electric kettle and the instant coffee. Tell them they have five minutes to do this.

3   While the students are doing the task, draw the Kitchen Plan on the board (unless you are using the OHT). After five or ten minutes, use this plan to feedback as a whole class on the best design for the kitchen.

4   Tell the students that your clients now want a report on the suggested improvements. Brainstorm which are the most important improvements and which are not so important. As students feedback, highlight their use of *should*, e.g. *You should move the fridge.*

5   Explain that the person who wrote Part 1 of the report is ill. The students must finish the report by writing Part 2. They can use the language in Part 1 to help them write Part 2. Write these cues on the board:

2 How to change the kitchen

2.1 You should move the fridge. The best place to put it is ... because ...

Give the pairs a few minutes to draft 2.1. Feedback onto the board and ask one student from each pair to copy this first section onto a piece of paper.

6   Tell the students, in pairs, to use this paper to continue with the report by writing the other three points, 2.2 to 2.4, based on their kitchen plan. Remind them how they prioritised the problems in step 4 and emphasise that the most important problems should be dealt with first.

7   After ten minutes, tell the pairs to swap their report with another pair. Ask them to read the report and decide how easy it is to understand and whether the improvements are logical. Ask them to award it a mark out of ten. Explain that the most logical report will win the contract. Feedback as a whole class and award the contract(s).

Follow up

● Ask the students to draw a plan of their own kitchens and analyse the layout. They can then write their own report for their parents or partner on how it can be improved.

● Tell the students to write a newspaper advertisement for their kitchen design company.

Report: Part 1

1 Problems with the kitchen

1.1 The fridge is big and stops the window opening. Also the oven is next to the fridge and the fridge does not work well when the oven is hot.

1.2 There are a lot of drawers for knives, forks and spoons but there is only one cupboard. It has plates, cups and saucepans in. There is not a cupboard for food.

1.3 There are not enough work surfaces, and the sink is full of washing-up.

1.4 It takes a long time to make a cup of coffee because the electric kettle, sugar and coffee are not in the same place.

Find the words in the report that mean these things:

1 A machine that keeps food cold   a   f _ _ _ _ _

2 A machine that cooks food   an   o_ _ _

3 Something you pull out and push in   a   d_ _ _ _ _

4 A place for water or the washing-up   a   s_ _ _

5 A machine that boils water   an   e_ _ _ _ _ _ _   k_ _ _ _ _

Kitchen Plan

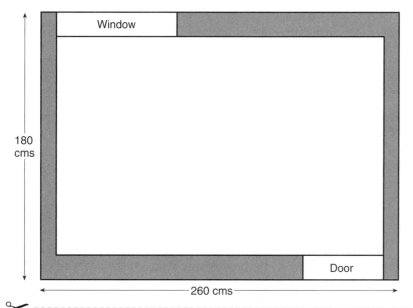

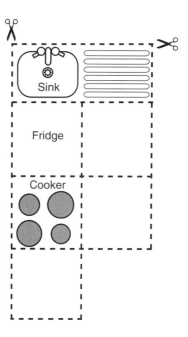

Possible Solution

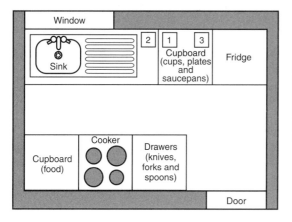

Key
1 coffee
2 kettle
3 sugar

4.2

Holiday house-swap

LEVEL
Intermediate

TOPIC
Houses, holidays

ACTIVITY TYPE
Matching, paired
simulation

**WRITING
FOCUS**
Personal letter
(descriptive); linking

TIME
50 minutes

KEY LANGUAGE
*to bump, coast, cosy,
on-street parking,
panoramic, pub,
spare bedroom,
suburb, water sports*

PREPARATION
One photocopy, cut up,
for each pair of
students

Optionally, one
photocopy of Writing
organisation 2 (p.124)
for each student

Warm up

1 Elicit the meaning of a holiday house-swap, i.e. a holiday anywhere in the world where you borrow someone else's house while they use yours.

2 Brainstorm the advantages and disadvantages of house-swaps.

3 Put the students in pairs and give each pair a copy of the Pictures and Notes. Tell them these are potential house-swaps which someone has made notes on. Tell them to match the notes to the pictures.

> **Answer key**
> 1 a 2 c 3 b 4 d

Main activity

1 Put the class into three groups, numbered 1–3. Ask them to only look at the house that has the same number as their group. Tell them to discuss whether they would like to stay in it.

2 Divide the groups into pairs and give each pair a copy of the Model Letter. Explain that it is a letter from the owner of one of the houses. Ask them to read it, match it to a house and circle the clues that helped them identify it.

> **Answer key**
> 4 (Clues: low doors, village, boat hire)

3 Ask the pairs to underline all the nouns and pronouns and draw arrows from the numbered pronouns to the nouns they refer to. Demonstrate how the first one has already been done. Feedback as a whole class.

> **Answer key**
> **1, 2, 3** home **4** doors **5** bathroom **6, 7** washing machine **8** pub

Discuss how these link the text together. Ask the students to find two more linking words in the last paragraph. (Answer: unfortunately, also)

4 Explain that in the three paragraphs the owner has tried to anticipate three questions that people might ask. Tell the pairs to write the questions. Feedback as a whole class.

> **Answer key**
> 1 What's special or different about the home?
> 2 Where are important things in the home?
> 3 Where are things in the surrounding area?

5 Ask the pairs to write a similar letter for the house they discussed in step 1. Tell them to ensure they answer the three questions from step 4, and use both the notes and the picture to help them write the letter.

6 When the students have written their letters, ask them to swap them with another pair from within their group. Ask them to check the letter for linkers and redraft it, if necessary, so that it flows more smoothly. You may want to give students a copy of Writing organisation 2 to help them with this (see p.124). Ask them also to correct any inaccurate information.

7 Ask the pairs to swap their letter with a pair from another group and decide if they would like to stay in the new house or not.

Follow up

• Ask the students to write a similar letter for their own home or a dream home.

• Ask the students to write a description of their home for an Internet house-swap site.

Pictures

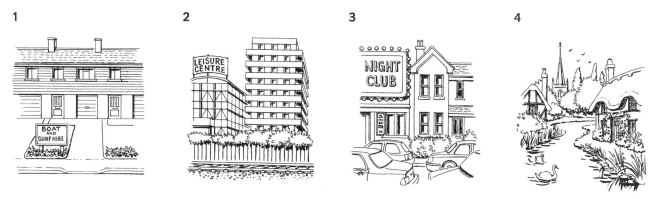

1   2   3   4

Notes

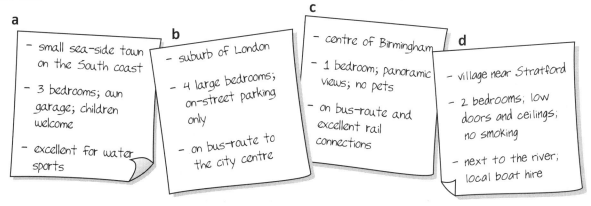

a
- small sea-side town on the South coast
- 3 bedrooms; own garage; children welcome
- excellent for water sports

b
- suburb of London
- 4 large bedrooms; on-street parking only
- on bus-route to the city centre

c
- centre of Birmingham
- 1 bedroom; panoramic views; no pets
- on bus-route and excellent rail connections

d
- village near Stratford
- 2 bedrooms; low doors and ceilings; no smoking
- next to the river; local boat hire

Model Letter

Honeysuckle Cottage
Beeton
Warwickshire WK3 4DB
24 October 2004

Dear Mr and Mrs Mann

I do hope you enjoy your stay in our home. You'll find ¹it's cosy but ²it's got everything you'll need. I don't know how tall you are, but ³it was built in 1558 and people were shorter then! Be careful of the doors – ⁴they're very low and it's easy to bump your head!

The bathroom's at the top of the stairs. ⁵It doesn't have much space to keep anything in but there are extra towels and sheets in the cupboard in the spare bedroom. If you need ⁶it, the washing machine's in the kitchen and ⁷it's quite easy to use. Washing powder's under the sink.

Unfortunately, there isn't a shop in the village but there's a supermarket in town. If you don't want to cook, the village pub does good food. ⁸It also does boat hire and the river is particularly pretty at this time of year.

Do contact me if you need further information.

Yours sincerely

Mrs Potter

4.3

The student house

LEVEL
Upper-intermediate

TOPIC
Rules, communal
living

ACTIVITY TYPE
Group role play

**WRITING
FOCUS**
Rules

TIME
50 minutes

KEY LANGUAGE
*housemates, to reach
a crisis, to set rules,
to share a house,
toiletries*;

Modals: *must, have to,
should, can,* etc.

PREPARATION
One set of Pictures, cut
up, for each group of
four students; one
copy of The Student
House for each student

Warm up

1   Divide the class into four groups, numbered 1–4. Give each group enough copies of the corresponding picture for one per student.

2   Ask the students to look at their picture and discuss: *What that person does in a typical day; What they think the person's bedroom is like; What the person normally cooks or eats.*

3   Write these cues on the board: *The most important thing in their life is …; They hate …; They love … .* Ask the students to write complete sentences about the person in their picture.

Main activity

1   Divide the groups into pairs and give each student a copy of The student house. Explain that the people in their pictures live together in a shared student house. Ask them to discuss and make notes on things that might cause problems or conflict between housemates in each of the rooms, e.g. who can use the bathroom first in the morning. Feedback as a whole class.

Suggested answer	
Bedroom **2** Loud music while they're trying to sleep **3** Noisy visitors **4** Other people taking their things	**Bathroom** **2** People leaving the bathroom dirty **3** Other people using their toiletries **4** People using all the hot water
Kitchen **2** Dividing the fridge between housemates **3** Others using their food **4** No-one washing up	**Lounge** **2** No-one keeping it tidy **3** People choosing favourite chairs **4** Smoking or non-smoking?

2   Put the students into new groups of four so that each new group has one student from each of the previous groups, i.e. 1–4. Ask them to each take on the role of the person in their picture and briefly explain to the others in the house what sort of person they are.

3   After ten minutes, stop the students and explain that the housemates are becoming increasingly annoyed with each other's lack of consideration. In fact, last night, there was a fight when someone refused to turn their music down. Tell the students to think of what their character might feel about it and the rules that they might want for the house. Split the groups into pairs and tell them to write a set of rules for the house. These should start with general rules but also include rules specific to each room.

4   After ten minutes, ask the groups to re-form to have a house meeting. They should try to redraft their two sets of rules into one which they can all agree on. Emphasise that each student pays money to live in the house and will not want to compromise over everything but nobody wants anybody to move out. If students cannot reach agreement on a rule, they should take a vote.

5   If you have enough time, display the rules around the classroom and ask students to walk around, read them and tick the house they would like to live in. Tell them not to tick their own. The writers of the most popular rules win!

Follow up

●   Ask the students to write advice for foreigners, which will be included in a travel book, about what they should do when staying in someone's home in your country.

●   Tell the students to use the points raised in their discussion to write an essay with this title: *'The most important rules for living'.*

Pictures

The Student House

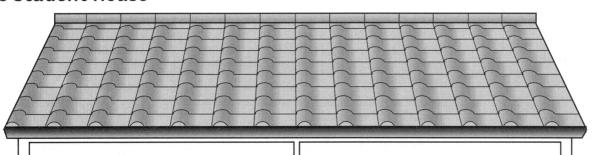

Bedroom	Bathroom
1 Keeping it a private space	1 Keeping other people waiting
2	2 ....
3	3 ....
4	4 ....
Kitchen	**Lounge**
1 Who cleans it?	1 TV: who controls it?
2	2 ....
3	3 ....
4	4 ....

5.1

Get lost!

LEVEL
Elementary

TOPIC
Directions,
relationships

ACTIVITY TYPE
Paired role play

**WRITING
FOCUS**
Personal letter
(giving directions)

TIME
50 minutes

KEY LANGUAGE
*gift, junction, past,
prison, roundabout,
rubbish dump,
to split up, traffic
lights;*
Prepositions of
location: *to go past a
place, to go over a
junction/crossroads, to
go through traffic
lights, on the right/left;*
imperatives

Note: The expression
Get lost! is a very
strong expression,
contradicting someone
and wishing them
elsewhere

PREPARATION
One photocopy, cut up,
for each pair of
students

Warm up

1 In pairs, give each pair a copy of the Map. As a whole class, brainstorm the meaning of difficult vocabulary, e.g. *rubbish dump, prison,* etc. and elicit or explain the words *crossroads, junction, roundabout* and *traffic lights.*

2 Explain that someone called Sue has written directions from the bus stop to her house. In pairs, tell the students to do the gap-fill exercise. After three minutes, feedback as a whole class.

> **Answer key**
> **2** bank   **3** traffic lights   **4** crossroads   **5** park   **6** junction

3 Read aloud the first sentence of the gap-fill. Write on the board: ~~You~~ *turn left at the roundabout.* Explain that the subject is omitted because this is an instruction that is true for anyone wanting to find Sue's house! Ask the students to find other examples of the imperative in the exercise. Use the map and the examples in the exercise to explain *to go past a place, to go over a crossroads* and *to go through traffic lights.* **Note:** *you'll see* is a prediction.

Main activity

1 Give each pair a copy of the Letter. Explain that it is a letter that gives directions for the same map but it has got wet and the ink has smudged. Ask the class to read the letter and then, as a whole class, brainstorm the relationship of the letter writer to the reader and its context, i.e. it is an ex-girlfriend or wife, replying to a letter from her former partner who requested a meeting.

2 Tell the pairs to complete the sentences that are smudged. After two or three minutes, feedback as a whole class.

> **Answer key**
> From the bus stop turn left at the **roundabout**. Go **straight past the bank** and **through the traffic lights**. Turn **right** at the crossroads. Pete's Cafe is on the left.

3 Elicit how the letter has got wet, i.e. Sue was crying as she wrote it. Elicit reasons why people split up. Explain that Sue is still upset with Steve. She is not going to send her original letter but write another one. Tell the pairs they can decide whether she directs Steve to a place where he can buy her a gift, e.g. the Chocolate Shop or a horrible place which shows how she really feels about him, e.g. the Rubbish Dump.

4 In pairs, tell the students to choose the place and write the new letter. Tell them they must not mention the final destination in their letter.

5 When the students have had enough time, tell them to swap their letter with another pair. Tell them to read the other pair's letter and find out where Steve finishes.

6 After five minutes, tell the pairs to join into groups of four and check if they are right about the finishing place. Tell them to discuss any directions that they found confusing and try to rewrite them.

Follow up

- Tell the students to write a letter giving directions from the nearest bus stop to their school, office or house.

- Explain that your neighbourhood or town has decided to make a 'Town Trail' leaflet to help tourists visit the three most interesting or historic local places on foot. Ask the students to write the leaflet, giving directions for a circular walk and brief descriptions of why the three places are interesting.

Map

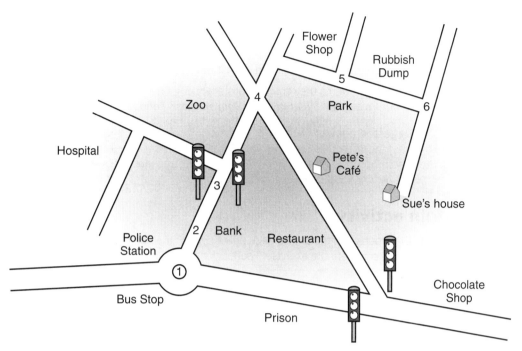

Sue has written directions to her house. Look at the numbers on the map and complete the directions:

Turn left at the **1** .roundabout. . Go past the **2** .... and then go through the

3 .... Go over the **4** .... Then turn right and go past the

5 .... on your right. At the **6** .... turn right, and you'll see

my house at the end of the street.

✂ -

Letter

Dear Steve

I was surprised to hear from you. I don't know how you got my new address. When we split up I told you I never wanted to see you again. A lot of things have happened since then. If you still want to talk, we can meet up at Pete's Café on Wednesday at 10.00. Just for a coffee!

You need to catch the number 25 bus to get there. Get off opposite the police station. From the bus stop turn left at the 🐾 🐾
Go   🐾   and 🐾
Turn   🐾   at the crossroads. Pete's Café is on the left.

I'll see you then.

Sue

5.2

The news on the street

LEVEL
Intermediate

TOPIC
Local newspapers

ACTIVITY TYPE
Text analysis,
group simulation

WRITING FOCUS
News article;
expanding notes

TIME
50 minutes

KEY LANGUAGE
*article, editor,
to edit/cut, ethnic,
headline, journalist,
lead, local, masthead,
quotation, summary,
target reader*

PREPARATION
One photocopy of the
Masthead for each
four students; one
photocopy of the
Sample Article for
each pair
Note: As an alternative
to the Warm up, bring
in copies of a local
newspaper and ask the
students to decide the
categories of news
it covers

Warm up

1   In groups of four, give each group a copy of the Masthead face down on the desk. Ask them to turn it over and brainstorm what it is.

2   Explain to the students they are journalists working on a new local weekly newspaper called *Your Voice*. Ask: *What interests your readers?* Feedback onto the board.

> **Suggested answer**
> local arts and sports; schools and clubs; local personalities and businesses; local transport and road safety; local shopping and jobs; environmental issues; local history; local politics; crime

Main activity

1   Split the groups into pairs. Give each pair a copy of the Sample Article and ask them to read it and complete the exercise. Feedback as a whole class.

> **Answer key**
> **a** 3   **b** 4   **c** 5   **d** 1   **e** 2

Elicit how the most important and interesting facts come first, the next most important facts second and so on down to part 5, which gives opinion.

2   Tell the students to turn the article upside down. Ask: *How is the article like a pyramid?*

> **Answer key**
> You can cut things away from the peak (sections 4 and 5) and it will still stand and make sense. If you take them from the base (sections 1, 2 and 3) it will collapse and make no sense.

Elicit how this structure helps the reader and the busy editor, i.e. it helps the reader decide whether they are interested in reading on and also the busy editor who can cut the last paragraphs if necessary to create space for other articles.

3   Give each group a target reader: young children; teenagers; young professionals; families; elderly people. Tell the groups they are journalists working for *Your Voice*. Ask them to use the areas of interest brainstormed in the Warm up and make notes about specific things in their own town that are of interest to their target reader.

4   Ask one person in every group to tear a piece of paper into four pieces and give one piece to each member of the group. Tell the students to each choose a different area of interest and write it on the paper with their notes. Ask them to fold it over so no-one can read it and pass it to the person on their right.

5   Brainstorm things that can happen in a community, e.g. a fire burns something, someone wins an award, someone steals something, etc. Write on the board the verbs only, i.e. *burns, wins, steals,* etc. Tell the students to choose one verb and write it on the folded paper and pass it, unopened, to the person on the right.

6   Tell the students to unfold their paper. In pairs, ask them to discuss how their verbs and notes could be linked. Encourage them to use their imagination. Tell the students to use the verb and notes as the basis for a short article modelled on the Sample Article's structure.

7   Ask the students to swap their articles and check them for organisation and whether they will appeal to their target reader.

Follow up

● Ask the students to research and write an article about a real local issue. The article should be no longer than 150 words and follow the structure of the sample article.

● Ask the students to find a newspaper or magazine that is obviously targeted at a youth audience. Explain that the newspaper or magazine wants to reposition itself and sell to young adults. Ask them to analyse the contents of the current issue and write recommendations on how the newspaper needs to change to appeal to the new target audience.

Masthead

15 November 2004

Your Voice Free

Reaching more readers in *your* area with the news you want to read

Sample Article

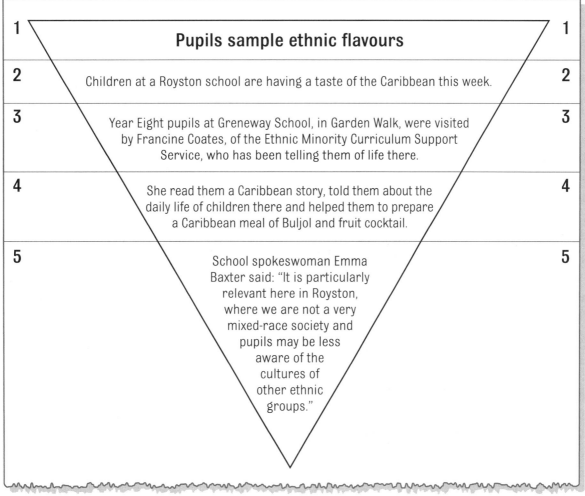

1 **Pupils sample ethnic flavours** 1

2 Children at a Royston school are having a taste of the Caribbean this week. 2

3 Year Eight pupils at Greneway School, in Garden Walk, were visited by Francine Coates, of the Ethnic Minority Curriculum Support Service, who has been telling them of life there. 3

4 She read them a Caribbean story, told them about the daily life of children there and helped them to prepare a Caribbean meal of Buljol and fruit cocktail. 4

5 School spokeswoman Emma Baxter said: "It is particularly relevant here in Royston, where we are not a very mixed-race society and pupils may be less aware of the cultures of other ethnic groups." 5

From *Royston Weekly News*, Thursday 30 May, 2002

Where are these things?
a a sentence that tells you who did things ....

b a sentence that tells you what they did ....

c a sentence that tells you why it was important ....

d the title or headline ....

e a short summary or lead ....

5.3

The big move

LEVEL
Upper-intermediate

TOPIC
Moving to the countryside

ACTIVITY TYPE
Paired role play

WRITING FOCUS
Personal letter (opinion); editing for emphasis

TIME
50 minutes

KEY LANGUAGE
to anticipate something, a cloud on the horizon, mother-in-law, pros and cons, to be in somebody's interest;

Modifiers: *so, really, completely, very, fairly, rather, such*; giving opinions

PREPARATION
One photocopy, cut up, for each student

Note: You may want to download more examples of problems and responses from www.problempages.co.uk

Warm up

1 Brainstorm what a problem page is, who writes to them and what they write about.

2 Give each student a copy of the Problem Page. Explain that it is from a parenting magazine. Tell the students they have five minutes to read it, find out what the problem is and whether they agree with the advice given. Feedback as a whole class.

Main activity

1 Ask the students to imagine that they are Charlotte. Explain that they have decided to take Annette's advice. Tell them, in pairs, they have five minutes to write the list of pros and cons.

2 After five minutes, give each student a copy of the Pros and Cons list and ask them to check it against their own and discuss any differences with their partner.

3 Write on the board: *In my opinion … .* Brainstorm other ways of expressing opinion, e.g. *I think that …; I really believe that …; It's possible that …; I'm sure that … .*

4 In their pairs, tell them they have ten minutes to write Charlotte's letter to Joyce, using some of the phrases brainstormed in step 3. After ten minutes, stop them and ask them to swap their letter with another pair.

5 Write on the board: *Life there will be better / much better / so much better for him.* Elicit how each modification increases the emphasis. Ask them to quickly reread the problem page and find any other phrases with similar modifiers.

> **Answer key**
> a really wonderful baby
> in Jack's very best interest

6 Give one copy of the Ways of Modifying exercise to each student. Ask them to list the phrases from weakest to most emphatic. Feedback as a whole class.

> **Answer key**
> **Adjectives:** 4, 3, 1, 2, 5
> **Adjective +noun:** d, b, c, a, e

7 In their pairs, ask the students to check and rewrite the new letter they swapped with another pair in step 4, using modifiers to add emphasis if they have not been used already.

8 If there is sufficient time, ask the students to swap back their letters and discuss in their pairs how persuasive the new draft is and whether it would change Joyce's mind.

Follow up

● Ask the students to write Joyce's reply to Charlotte's letter.

● Explain that Joyce has written to the problem page. Tell the students to write Annette's advice to her concerning Charlotte's decision to move.

Problem Page

Ask Annette — The page where your parenting problems are answered

Dear Annette

We're so lucky to have a really wonderful baby called Jack. We still can't believe it and he's nearly a month old now!

The only cloud on the horizon is our big move. Our house is too small for a family and we've decided to move out of London so that Jack can have all the benefits of growing up in the country. Life there will be so much better for him.

The problem is that my mother-in-law, Joyce, doesn't know yet and when she finds out she'll go mad. Jack's her only grandchild and she expects to see him every day. What should we do?

Charlotte Hipkin, London W5

Annette says ...

Don't worry Charlotte, it may take a little time but Joyce will understand. If you can't face telling her, write her a letter.

Try to anticipate some of the arguments she'll use against you. Make a list of pros and cons for the move and use some of your most positive points in the letter.

If you explain your decision is in Jack's very best interest, I'm sure she'll begin to understand your way of thinking.

Pros

+ we'll all have a more relaxed lifestyle
+ houses are cheaper: we'll all have more space
+ less pollution, cleaner air
+ nice to live in a small, friendly community
+ less crime
+ Jack can explore the countryside without fear of danger

Cons

- not close to family, especially Joyce
- not close to supportive friends and all the other new mums I know
- poor public transport: I'll need a car
- far from a supermarket / big shops
- not close to a hospital in an emergency
- fewer organised things to do (no cinemas, night-clubs, etc)

Ways of Modifying

Gradable adjective

Neutral phrase: It's good.

1 It's *really / very* good.
2 It's *very / really* very good.
3 It's *rather* good.
4 It's *fairly* good.

Gradable adjective + noun

Neutral phrase: It's a good place.

a It's really *a very / such a* very good place.
b It's *a very / such a* good place.
c It's really *a very / such a* good place.
d It's a *fairly* good place.

Non-gradable adjective

Neutral phrase: It's excellent.

5 It's *absolutely / really* excellent.

Non-gradable adjective + noun

Neutral phrase: It's an excellent place.

e It's a(n) *absolutely/really* excellent place.

6.1

Wish you were here ...

LEVEL
Elementary

TOPIC
Holiday problems

ACTIVITY TYPE
Text analysis

WRITING FOCUS
Postcard

TIME
50 minutes

KEY LANGUAGE
bistro, city break, cruise, journey, night-life, noisy, romantic, thunderstorm, trendy;

Omission of pronouns, articles and auxiliary verbs

PREPARATION
One photocopy, cut up, for each pair of students

Note: To help students with step 5, you may want to download other official tourist websites worldwide via www.123world.com/tourist/index.html

Warm up

As a whole class, brainstorm different types of holiday. Ask: *Has anyone been on a City Break? Why did they choose it and what did they enjoy about it?*

> **Suggested answer**
> easy to get to; easy to get around; visiting important places; good cafés; excellent shopping, etc.

Main activity

1   Put students in pairs. Give each pair a copy of the Postcard. Write on the board: *Where are Wendy and Steve? Are they enjoying their holiday? What have they done?* Ask the pairs to write their answers while you copy the postcard onto the board. As a whole class, feedback and check difficult vocabulary.

2   Ask the students to look at the postcard on the board. Explain that some words are omitted and indicate their location using the ^ symbol used in the First draft checklist, (p.120), e.g. ^ *Having a great time.* When you have indicated all the omissions, ask the students what is missing from the first sentence – *We are* having a great time. Discuss why it has been shortened, i.e. because it is quicker for the holidaymaker who has a lot of postcards to write and it means they can fit more onto the card.

3   Brainstorm the other words that have been omitted (i.e. subject pronouns and auxiliary verbs) and add them to the postcard.

> **Suggested answer**
> **We are** having a great time. **We had a** good journey and **the** weather **is** mostly good. **It is** sometimes a little wet. **The** hotel **is** right in **the** city centre! **It is** great for the Eiffel Tower. **We** shopped all yesterday **and** got some really trendy clothes. **The** food **is** excellent (**we have** tried lots of different bistros). **I** am really looking forward to our dinner cruise on the River Seine tomorrow evening – **it is / will be** really romantic!

4   Brainstorm what can go wrong on holiday. In the same pairs, give each pair a copy of the Holiday Problems. Tell them one of the pictures shows a problem Wendy and Steve had. Ask them to reread the postcard and decide which picture shows their problem. Feedback as a whole class (Answer: 4). Elicit what Wendy wrote about the weather and what she really meant. Write on the board: ☹*Weather bad*→ ☺*Weather mostly good / not too good / a little bad.* Explain that the weather is bad in all the descriptions but the ☺ sentences describe it in a more positive way. Ask: *Why didn't she say more about their problem in the postcard?* (Answer: because she does not want people to worry about whether they are enjoying themselves; she wants people to feel positive about their holiday.)

5   Ask the students to think of a city they would like to visit. Tell them to imagine a holiday in that city and ask them to write a postcard home to their parents or partner. Explain that they can decide if they are having a good time or a bad time and whether there are any problems. Emphasise that they want people at home to think they are having a good time. If there are any problems they should not lie, but make them sound a little more positive than they really are by using phrases such as *not too ...*, *mostly* and *a little*.

6   Ask the students to swap their postcards with another student and guess where the sender is and whether there are any problems or not.

Follow up

*   Explain to the students that they have met someone on holiday and done lots of romantic things together. Tell them to write two postcards: one to their parents or grandparents and the other to their best friend. Emphasise that they should think carefully about what to include and what to omit in each card!

*   Ask the students to rewrite their postcard as a letter, including all the words they have omitted.

Postcard

Having a great time. Good journey
and weather mostly good.
Sometimes a little wet. Hotel
right in city centre! Great for
the Eiffel Tower. Shopped all
yesterday: got some really
trendy clothes. Food excellent
(tried lots of different bistros!).
Am really looking forward to our
dinner cruise on the River Seine
tomorrow evening – really
romantic!

Love, Wendy (and Steve)

Holiday Problems

1

2

FLIGHT 401 DELAYED

3

HOTEL

4

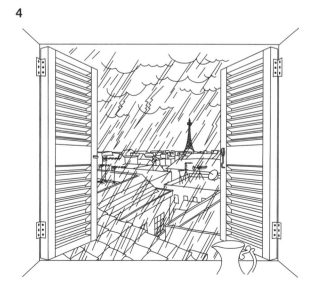

6.2

Paradise tours

LEVEL
Intermediate

TOPIC
Choosing package
holidays

ACTIVITY TYPE
Matching, text
analysis

**WRITING
FOCUS**
Brochure description;
targeting audience

KEY LANGUAGE
*extras, holidaymakers,
luggage handling,
military tattoo,
package holiday,
pick-up, resort, singles,
thrill, topped up*;

Non-gradable
adjectives, e.g.
*fantastic, magnificent,
perfect*

TIME
50 minutes

PREPARATION
One photocopy for
each pair of students

Warm up

1   Explain that you want a holiday, you want to choose it from a brochure and you want flights and accommodation arranged for you. Elicit that this is a *package holiday.* Brainstorm the students' ideal package holidays. Ask: *What extras should be included? Do your parents or partners enjoy the same kind of holiday as you?*

2   In pairs, give each pair a copy of the photocopiable page. Ask them to read the descriptions of Malia and Edinburgh and decide which of the holidaymakers in the pictures the different descriptions are targeted at. Feedback as a whole class, eliciting how the writer of the brochure descriptions has focused on the benefits of each holiday for one particular target audience, i.e. Malia is described in such a way as to appeal to young single people whereas the description of Edinburgh emphasises what it has to offer for older people.

Main activity

1   Draw a horizontal line on the board with a smiley face at one end and a sad face at the other. Ask the students to copy this. Write these adjectives on the board and ask them to put them at the right place on the line: *very bad, perfect, appalling, very good, good, bad, okay.* Feedback as a whole class and elicit how *perfect* and *appalling* represent the extremes.

2   Tell the students to underline the adjectives in the description of Edinburgh. As a whole class, discuss how the brochure is selling an image of the ideal holiday for that particular target audience, and therefore many of these adjectives represent positive extremes, e.g. *magnificent, exquisite, stunning,* etc. Brainstorm six more adjectives that represent positive extremes.

3   Elicit what is missing from the first sentence in the description of Edinburgh and why, i.e. the subject, in order to emphasise the verb and what you *can* do.

4   In the same pairs, ask the students to make notes on what they would add or change to target the description at young single people, e.g. more of an emphasis on night-life, sports and more active leisure activities. Feedback as a whole class.

5   Ask the students to write a similar description of their own town for a package holiday brochure. Tell them to choose a specific target audience: young single people; couples with children; older people. Emphasise that they must target their description appropriately and decide on what free extras will be included.

6   When they have had sufficient time, ask the students to join with another pair and swap brochure descriptions. Tell them to read the new description and discuss what type of tourist the description is targeted at. Ask them to check with the writers of the description and then suggest anything that could be altered to make it more appealing to the target audience.

Follow up

●   Ask the students to write some descriptions of excursions which tour company representatives can give to tourists who have just arrived in the students' home town. They must be targeted at one particular audience.

●   Ask the students to write a more critical entry for their town for a travel guide book targeted at the business traveller.

Brochure Descriptions

Malia, Crete

CRETE

Brilliant beaches and fantastic clubs to keep all you 'party animals' happy. There's loads going on: try the amazing Waterpark or our great jet-skis. Every night is party night on the white, white sand. The best DJs and the best music make Malia the place to be this summer! This is definitely the perfect resort for sun, fun and more fun!!! The partying doesn't even have to stop for food: whatever your taste, Greek, British, Indian, Mexican, Chinese, local restaurants and bistros will keep you topped up at amazingly low prices. And our singles accommodation means no crying kids or old people to complain about you.

You can also book diving or snorkelling lessons at a small additional cost, go horse-riding or visit the ruins of an ancient palace.

Free extras: *Just in case you forget – every holidaymaker gets a free beach towel, barbecue and camera to record all those unforgettable moments!*

Edinburgh, Scotland

Edinburgh, Scotland

Relax in Royal Edinburgh, the capital of Scotland, with its magnificent castle and the beautiful squares of the New Town. Our exclusive 5-star hotel is ideally located for the best shops, museums and galleries in the country and is in easy reach of all the major attractions of the city. No need for taxis: we give you world-famous arts festivals and the military tattoo on the doorstep. Have a relaxing morning viewing Scotland's exquisite Crown Jewels at the castle and spend the afternoon listening to a string quartet in the hotel's own elegant ballroom. Guests can also choose from many additional organised excursions: visit the Royal Yacht Britannia at the Ocean Terminal, experience the thrill of making your own glass at the Edinburgh Crystal Visitor Centre or take a coach trip into the stunning Scottish Highlands.

Free extras: From the moment you leave home you can relax. We arrange the pick-up and provide luxury coach travel direct to your hotel. We provide a complete luggage handling service so you don't need to worry about carrying heavy cases, and our tour manager is on hand 24 hours a day for your peace of mind.

Holidaymakers

1

2

3

6.3

FAQs: Frequently Asked Questions

LEVEL
Upper-intermediate

TOPIC
Transport advice

ACTIVITY TYPE
Paired text analysis

WRITING FOCUS
Website; targeting audience

TIME
50 minutes

KEY LANGUAGE
budget traveller, destination, fare, to recognise something, route

PREPARATION
One photocopy for each student

Note: If your class contains solely Turkish students, omit Warm up step 1; if your class contains a few Turkish students, omit Warm up step 1 and ask them to explain to the class what a dolmuş is and how you use it

Warm up

1 Brainstorm what students know about Turkey. Write the word *dolmuş* on the board. (The *ş* in *dolmuş* is pronounced *sh*.) Explain that a dolmuş is similar to a bus and is used a lot in Turkey.

2 Tell the students they are going to read a FAQs, Frequently Asked Questions, web page about taking a dolmuş. Brainstorm who its target audience will probably be, i.e. the budget foreign traveller. In pairs, tell the students they have five minutes to write a list of questions they think will be answered on the website.

Main activity

1 Give out one copy of the Travel FAQs page per student. Explain the questions are missing. Tell them to read it and find out how many of their questions are answered. After five minutes, feedback as a whole class.

2 In pairs, tell the students to reread the page and complete the gaps with the six missing questions. After five minutes, feedback as a whole class.

> **Suggested answer**
> 1 What is a dolmuş?
> 2 Why take a dolmuş?
> 3 How do I catch a dolmuş?
> 4 How do I pay?
> 5 What should I do and what shouldn't I do on a dolmuş?
> 6 How long will I have to wait for a dolmuş?

3 Explain that they are going to write a FAQs page for foreigners about transport in the town or country where they are studying. Split the class into two groups, A and B. Tell group A, in pairs, to brainstorm a list of questions that budget travellers would want answered on a FAQs page, e.g. questions on hitch-hiking, bus and rail travel. Tell group B, in pairs, to brainstorm a list of questions that business travellers would want answered, e.g. questions on internal flights, car hire and taxis.

4 After five minutes tell the students to swap lists with a pair from the other group. Tell them to prioritise the new list, edit the questions down to a maximum of six and to write the FAQs page.

5 When the students have had sufficient time, tell them to swap their FAQs page with a pair from the other group. Tell them to read the new FAQs page and decide how helpful it will be to the target audience. Give the students some time to feedback to each other.

Follow up

- Tell the students to list customs and taboos in their country about either visiting a religious place or attending a formal dinner party. Tell them to choose either the budget or business traveller and write a FAQs page which will help them in one of these situations.

- Ask the students to write a more general visitor advice FAQs page for their town or region, targeted at holidaymakers.

Web Page

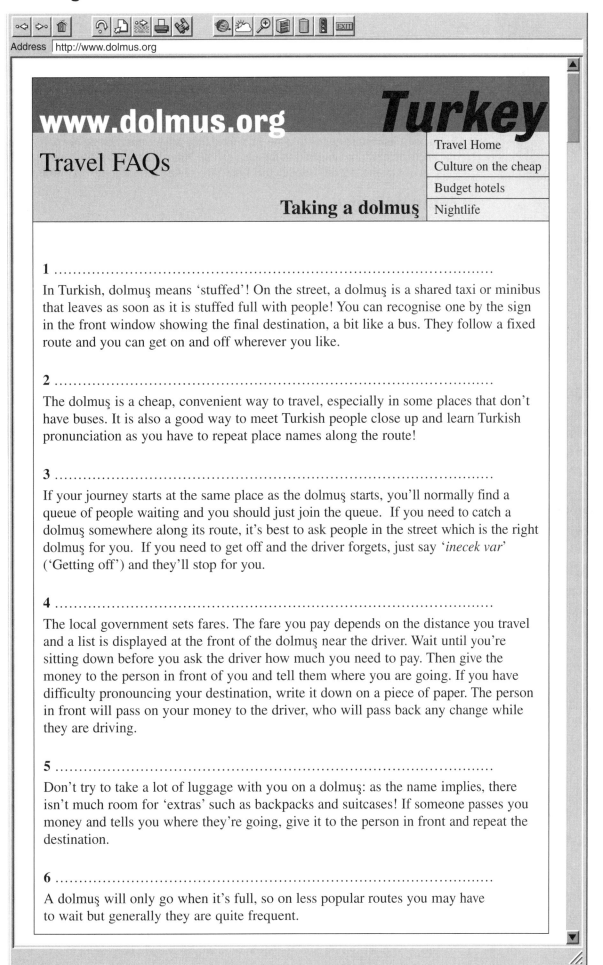

A lovely meal

LEVEL
Elementary

TOPIC
Dinner parties

ACTIVITY TYPE
Simulation

WRITING FOCUS
Personal letter (descriptive)

TIME
50 minutes

KEY LANGUAGE
burnt, dessert,
to be off, menu,
main course, spicy,
starter, sweet,
tasteless,
tasty, undercooked;
Adjectives; *so/ because*

PREPARATION
One photocopy for each student

Warm up

1 Explain to the students that they are going to have a dinner party. Write on the board: *Starter / Main Course / Dessert*. Brainstorm different food for each course, e.g. starter – chicken soup; main course – spaghetti bolognese; dessert – ice cream.

2 In pairs, ask the students to write what food they will have at their dinner party. Ask them to put at least one type of dish for each course. After five minutes, ask them to swap their menu with another pair. Explain that they have invited the other pair to the dinner.

Main activity

1 Tell the students that they went to the other pair's dinner party and are now going to describe it. Give each student a copy of the photocopiable page. Ask them to look at the pairs of adjectives, which can all be used to describe food. Check any difficult vocabulary, and explain that the pairs of adjectives show first negative and then positive opinions of food; the one exception is d, where both the adjectives are negative – *well-cooked* is the positive form.

2 In pairs, ask them to do Part 1 of the Adjectives exercise. Explain that the first one has been done for them. After three minutes feedback as a whole class.

> **Suggested answer**
> 1 a, b (in colloquial English c is also possible!);
> 2 a, c, d, e, g
> 3 a, c, d, e, g
> 4 a, c, d, e, g
> 5 a, b, c, d, f, g

3 Write these sentences on the board: *The meat was too spicy because they used too much chilli pepper. The soup was too tasteless, so I didn't eat it.* Highlight the cause and the effect in each and then elicit similar sentences using *so* and *because*.

4 In pairs, ask the students to do Part 2 of the Adjectives exercise. Feedback as a whole class.

> **Suggested answer**
> 2 beautiful / tasty / just right / fresh
> 3 terrible/tasteless/burnt
> 4 beautiful / tasty / just right / fresh
> 5 terrible / because the cream was off

5 Explain to the students that they are going to write to a friend describing the dinner party they went to. They must say it was either really good or really terrible, and give reasons why things were good or bad, using *so* and *because*. They should use the Letter Template and the menu they were given in the Warm up.

6 After ten minutes, ask the students to swap their letter with their partner. Ask them to read the new letter and decide: *if they think the meal was good or bad; if their partner explains well why things were good or bad.* Tell them to underline any reasons that they think are not good reasons.

7 When they have had enough time, ask them to swap back their letters and rewrite anything that has been underlined.

8 If there's time, ask them to join with the pair who invited them to dinner in the Warm up. Ask the two pairs to swap letters. Explain they have found the letters by accident. Tell them to read the letters and decide if they will invite these people to a dinner party again!

Follow up

● Ask the students to write a letter to a friend describing the best or worst meal they have ever had in real life.

● Ask the students to write a letter accepting or rejecting a second invitation to dinner at the same place, giving a polite reason as to why they do or don't want to go.

Adjectives

a terrible/beautiful
b boring/interesting
c tasteless/tasty
d burnt/undercooked
e too spicy / just right
f too sweet / just right
g off/fresh

Part 1: Put these adjectives in the correct box. Some can go in more than one box.

1 People	2 Fish	3 Meat	4 Vegetables	5 Dessert
a, b				

Part 2: Complete each sentence with one adjective from Part 1.

1 The person next to me was ...._boring_................. , so I moved.
2 The fish was .... , so I ate it all.
3 The meat was .... because they forgot it was in the oven.
4 The vegetables were .... , so I asked for more.
5 The dessert was .... because ....

Letter Template

> Dear _____
>
> I went to a beautiful/terrible dinner party yesterday. It was really good/bad! It was at
> _____ house. The other guests were _____
> because they talked about _____ all night.
> The food was really _____
> _____
> _____
> _____
>
> If you get an invite to their next dinner party, you must/mustn't accept!
>
> Love
>
> _____

7.2

The Greasy Spoon

LEVEL
Intermediate

TOPIC
Restaurant hygiene

ACTIVITY TYPE
Paired spot-the-difference, text analysis

WRITING FOCUS
Report

KEY LANGUAGE
food poisoning,
hygiene,
health hazard;
The passive voice

TIME
50 minutes

PREPARATION
One photocopy, cut up, for each pair of students

Optionally, one photocopy of Writing style 1 (p.125) for each student

Warm up

1   Mime drinking something, holding your stomach in agony and then collapsing. Ask: *What has happened?* Elicit the noun *poison*. Alternatively, ask: *How can food make you sick?*

2   Ask: *What is food poisoning? What causes it?* Elicit the vocabulary *hygiene* and *a health hazard*, and examples, e.g. *washing your hands* and *a dirty kitchen*.

Main activity

1   Divide the class into two groups, A and B. Explain that they are inspectors who are responsible for hygiene in restaurants. Give each student a copy of The Restaurant Kitchen picture that corresponds to their group's letter. Ask them to discuss the kitchen picture in their groups and write down five visible health hazards.

2   Pair the students, so that each pair contains a student from both groups. Explain that they visited the same restaurant on two different days. Ask them not to show each other their pictures but to describe the health hazards they saw and take notes on what their partner saw.

3   Tell the students that they have to write a report. Give each pair a copy of the Report Template. Explain that the first two sections have been written for them. Elicit how the report is structured and brainstorm what to include in the sections headed *Main Findings, Conclusion* and *Recommendations*.

4   Tell them to discuss in pairs what health hazards there might be in the dining area and toilets and add sub-section headings to 3.2 and 3.3, e.g. *3.2.1 Dirty tables, mice infestation*, etc. Feedback as a whole class.

5   Ask the students to underline the verbs in the Summary and Introduction. Elicit how the passive voice is used in the Summary to emphasise what happened and what must change and the active in the Introduction to explain who did what. Brainstorm whether active or passive verbs should be used in the other sections.

> **Suggested answer**
> **3** a mixture   **4** passive   **5** active

6   In pairs, tell the students to complete the report on a separate piece of paper.

7   When they have had sufficient time, ask them to swap their report with another pair. Ask them to check the other pair's report for style and meaning and underline anything that they feel is too informal or does not make sense. You may want to give students a copy of Writing style 1 to help them with this (see p.125). After five minutes, ask them to swap back their reports and redraft them if necessary.

Follow up

●   Ask the students to take the role of the restaurant owner and write the letter to the Health Inspectors, using the passive where appropriate, to explain what action they have taken to improve things.

●   Ask the students to take the role of a disgusted customer who has seen the kitchen. Tell them to write the letter of complaint.

The Restaurant Kitchen

A

B

Report Template

Health Inspector's Report on the Greasy Spoon Restaurant, Cambridge

1 Summary

During two recent inspections of the Greasy Spoon Restaurant, Cambridge, it was found to be a serious health hazard. After each inspection the restaurant was immediately closed and not allowed to reopen until repairs had been made and its staff trained in basic food hygiene. It is disturbing that the café was allowed to get into such a state on two separate occasions and further action may need to be taken in future to protect the public.

2 Introduction

The Greasy Spoon, owned by Mr E. Coli, is a small café which serves traditional English food. We carried out the inspections on 10 July and 16 December 2004. On both occasions we found serious problems and immediately closed the café. The café reopened after follow up inspections proved Mr E. Coli had satisfactorily dealt with the outstanding health hazards.

3 Main Findings

3.1 The kitchen

3.2 The dining area

3.3 The customer toilets

4 Conclusion

5 Recommendations

7.3

Black or white?

LEVEL
Upper-intermediate

TOPIC
Marketing coffee

ACTIVITY TYPE
Group simulation

WRITING FOCUS
Advertising copy; expanding notes

TIME
50 minutes

KEY LANGUAGE
aroma, clear conscience, commodity, compromise, profit, slogan, target audience/ market, to trade, USP (Unique Selling Proposition)

PREPARATION
One photocopy, cut up, for each pair of students

Note: If you wish, photocopy a magazine advertisement and use it as a model that students can analyse before doing the Main activity

More support material for Fairtrade can be found at www.fairtrade.org.uk

Warm up

1   Write on the board: *Black or white?* Brainstorm what the context for this question is. Answer: This is an expression used in Great Britain for asking if you want milk in your coffee. (**Note:** there is also a secondary meaning – a *black-and-white issue* is one where it is easy to decide what is right or wrong.)

2   Ask the students what they know about coffee and how it is processed. In pairs, give each pair a copy of the Coffee Break Quiz and tell them they have three minutes to decide if the statements are true or false. Feedback as a whole class.

> **Answer key**
> **1** F (it came from Ethiopia)   **2** T (oil is the first)   **3** F (it earns 75%)   **4** T   **5** T   **6** T

As a whole class, discuss who you think has most power in the coffee-trade – the growers or the buyers?

Main activity

1   Explain that the students work for an advertising agency. They have been given the brief of promoting a new product: *Fairtrade* instant coffee. Give each pair a copy of the Advertising Brief. Tell the students to read it and answer these questions: *How is Fairtrade coffee different to its competitors? Who buys it? Why?* Feedback as whole class.

2   Explain that the advertising campaign is to run in three very different magazines, targeted at: trendy young adults; couples with children; older people (60+). Each magazine will need a different type of advertisement but they will all use the same slogan. Join the pairs into groups of four, and tell the students to choose a slogan from the Advertising Brief or write one themselves that they think will appeal to all three markets.

3   Give different groups different target markets, ensuring that the other students do not hear. Tell them they have 20 minutes to design a full-page magazine advertisement aimed at that target. The advertisement must include: a catchy headline; about 75 words 'selling' the product; the slogan from step 2; a logo. It can also make use of the quotations from coffee growers. They must ensure the target market buys *Fairtrade* coffee, rather than the coffee of its competitors, by highlighting how it is unique (this is known as creating a USP – Unique Selling Proposition). Elicit how they can do this by emphasising the benefits to the consumer that arise from the selling points (known as FAB – Features and Benefits).

4   After twenty minutes stop them and tell each group to nominate one person to be its 'ambassador' to another group. Tell the ambassador to take their group's advertisement to another group.

5   Tell the new group to read the new advertisement and decide which market it is aimed at and how it could be improved. During the discussion the ambassador must stay silent but should take notes.

6   After five minutes, tell the ambassadors to return to their groups with their own advertisement and explain to the group what improvements need to be made. The group should then redraft their advertisement.

7   If there is time, ask each group to present its advertisement to the class. The class should then vote on which advertisement they think will most appeal to each target market.

Follow up

- Tell the students to find an advertisement in a magazine and write an analysis of it describing the product's selling points, benefits, target market and how successful they feel it is.

- Tell the students to write a discursive essay with this title: '*If people really wanted ethically produced products, they would already be buying them. Discuss.*'

Coffee Break Quiz

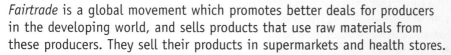

Are these statements TRUE or FALSE?

1 Coffee originally came from Brazil. ☐

2 Coffee is the second most valuable commodity traded in the world. ☐

3 Uganda earns 30% of its foreign income from coffee. ☐

4 Coffee can be sold over 150 times before it reaches the supermarket shelf and each time someone makes a profit. ☐

5 Seven million farmers, 70 per cent of coffee growers, farm 50,000m^2 of land or less. ☐

6 Six multinational companies now buy over 60% of coffee exports. ☐

 -

Advertising Brief

FAIRTRADE COFFEE

FAIRTRADE
Guarantees
a better deal
for Third World
Producers

Background

Fairtrade is a global movement which promotes better deals for producers in the developing world, and sells products that use raw materials from these producers. They sell their products in supermarkets and health stores.

Selling points	Benefits	Target market	Media
Poor growers get a fair price for their produce	– a clearer conscience	– people who are concerned about social issues	national magazines
Most growers use fewer chemicals	– better health	– people who want natural products	
Only the best quality coffee beans are used	– excellent flavour and aroma	– people who appreciate quality	

Possible slogans

1 Coffee with a conscience   2 Quality without compromise

Your slogan: ....

Quotations from coffee growers

Before *Fairtrade* coffee:

"There is total insecurity because you are completely dependent on the coffee price. There is a terrible rising and falling of the price."

- Manuel Alos Pancho, Colombia
  (source: The Fairtrade Foundation)

Now:

"Now I have money to buy clothes for my children."

- Mario Hernandez, Nicaragua
  (source: Cafédirect)

8.1

Virtually friends

LEVEL
Elementary

TOPIC
Internet friendships

ACTIVITY TYPE
Matching, paired
role play

**WRITING
FOCUS**
Personal e-mail

TIME
50 minutes

KEY LANGUAGE
Adjectives describing
people's physical
appearance: *curly,
dark, fair, freckled, full,
large, long, pointed,
short, small, straight,
wide, etc.; pen pal, to
get on with (someone)*

PREPARATION
One photocopy, cut up,
for each pair of
students

Note: You may want to
follow this activity with
class e-mail exchanges.
Visit www.iecc.org
for contacts

Warm up

1   Draw a circle, square and oval on the board and elicit the adjectives of shape we can use
for faces: *round, square* and *oval*.

2   Ask: *Can you describe your face?* Elicit different adjectives to describe facial features and
write them on the board, ensuring you include these: *fair, dark, short, shoulder-length,
long, curly, straight, small, large, full, narrow.*

3   Put the students in pairs and give each pair a copy of the Face. Ask the pairs to discuss
which adjectives on the board describe which facial feature and write them in the correct
box. Explain that the adjectives of shape have already been completed as an example.
After five minutes, feedback as a whole class.

> **Suggested answer**
> **Eyes:** small, large
> **Hair:** fair, dark, short, shoulder-length, long, curly, straight
> **Lips:** full, narrow
> **Nose:** small, large, long

Main activity

1   In the same pairs, give one copy of the E-mail to each pair and explain that it was written
by Anne, who has just met her Internet pen pal for the first time. She is writing to her
brother, Dave. Tell the students to answer these questions: *Do you think Anne liked her?
Do you think now they've met they're going to be real friends? Why / Why not?* Feedback
as a whole class, eliciting how Anne has been disappointed in the way her pen pal has
behaved and has described her in negative terms. Elicit how it could be made more
neutral by cutting the reference to a horse!

2   Highlight the differences between an e-mail and a personal letter, i.e. there is a subject line;
when an e-mail is part of an ongoing dialogue and the recipient is a close friend or relative
no opening or closing formula is necessary; e-mails tend to be much briefer than letters.

3   In pairs, ask the students to look at the Pen Pal pictures and decide which person Anne
met. (Answer: Suzie)

4   In pairs, ask the students to choose one of the other pictures. Explain that they must
imagine that this person is their Internet pen pal. Write on the board: *What does he/she
look like? What did he/she do when you met him/her? Do you like him/her?* Tell them to
write an e-mail to a relative describing the meeting. The e-mail must include answers to
the three questions.

5   Tell the students to swap their e-mail with another pair. Explain that they must read the
new e-mail, decide which person is being described and whether the new Internet pen
pals are going to be friends.

Follow up

*   Ask the students to imagine they met a famous person. Ask them to write a similar e-mail
to Anne's, describing what happened at the meeting and what the person looked like
close up. Tell them to swap their e-mail with another pair and guess who the person is.

*   Tell the students to write Suzie's diary entry for the day of the meeting.

Face

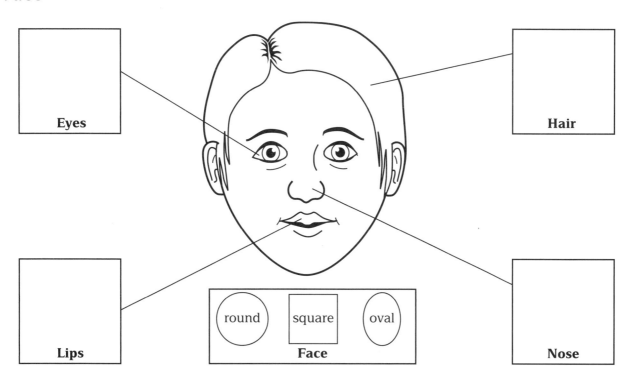

Eyes

Hair

round   square   oval
Face

Lips

Nose

✂ --

E-mail

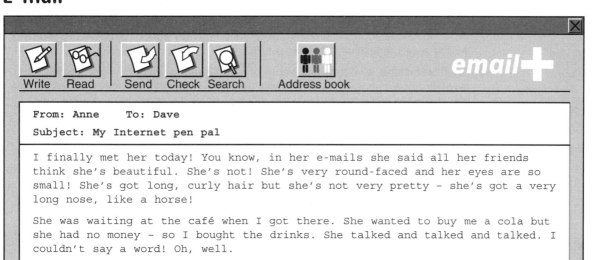

Write   Read   Send   Check   Search   Address book   *email*➕

From: Anne   To: Dave
Subject: My Internet pen pal

I finally met her today! You know, in her e-mails she said all her friends
think she's beautiful. She's not! She's very round-faced and her eyes are so
small! She's got long, curly hair but she's not very pretty – she's got a very
long nose, like a horse!

She was waiting at the café when I got there. She wanted to buy me a cola but
she had no money – so I bought the drinks. She talked and talked and talked. I
couldn't say a word! Oh, well.

I think we're going to get on but I don't know. She seemed okay. Let me know
what you think!

✂ --

Pen Pals

Becky   Nicola   Suzie   James   Rob   Mike

8.2

Business contacts

LEVEL
Intermediate

TOPIC
Meeting business
contacts

ACTIVITY TYPE
Text analysis

**WRITING
FOCUS**
Business e-mail

TIME
50 minutes

KEY LANGUAGE
Adjectives of body
shape: *beefy, muscular,
muscle-bound,
overweight, plump,
skinny, slim,* etc.;
adjectives of
personality: *arrogant,
bullying, clear-sighted,
confident, impatient,
persuasive, self-
contained,* etc.;
external, internal

PREPARATION
One photocopy, cut up,
for each pair of
students

Optionally, one
photocopy of Writing
style 1 (p.125) for each
student

Warm up

1 Divide the board in half. Write on one side *Body shape* and the other *Personality*.
Brainstorm adjectives to describe body shape, e.g. *thin, tall, short,* etc and personality, e.g.
shy, confident, careful, etc. and elicit if each has a positive, negative or neutral meaning.

2 In pairs, give each pair a copy of Ways of Describing People and ask to complete the
exercise. Feedback as whole class.

> **Answer key**
> **a** plump   **b** skinny   **c** beefy   **d** forceful   **e** arrogant   **f** shy

Main activity

1 Explain that you are going to give the students an internal company e-mail from a
manager to a more junior employee. It describes a difficult customer that the employee
does not know. Ask: *Is the description likely to be positive, neutral or negative?*

2 Give each pair a copy of E-mail 1. Ask them to read the e-mail to check if they were right.
Ask them to underline any negative or neutral adjectives used in the description. Feedback
as whole class. Elicit how it is quite informal as it is an internal e-mail and Petra Halliday
expresses her opinions candidly. Highlight phrases which she uses to show how first
appearances can be deceptive, e.g. *he appears …, don't be fooled …, he may look … .*

3 Ask the students to write Mr Beynon's e-mail to Paul Simmons, giving his flight details
(flight number and ETA) and information on how he can recognise him at the airport. Elicit
how it is likely to be more formal, as it is an external e-mail and Mr Beynon has never met
Paul, and how it will differ in content, i.e. he will not discuss his personality and is likely to
be more positive about his physical appearance. You may want to give students a copy of
Writing style 1 to help with this (see p.125).

4 After five minutes, give each pair a copy of E-mail 2 and tell them to check it against their
own. Elicit how it shows greater formality than E-mail 1 in its lack of abbreviations and the
use of an opening and closing formula, and how it has also been sent/copied to Petra
Halliday, i.e. the use of Cc.

5 In pairs, ask each pair to think of a famous person and write two lists of adjectives: one
that could describe that person's body shape and another for their personality. Tell them
to write an e-mail to a colleague, asking them to meet that person at the airport. Tell them
to decide whether to be positive, negative or neutral in their description of that person.

6 When they have had enough time, ask them to join with another pair to make a group of
four. Ask them to swap their e-mails, read the other pair's and decide who is being
described and if it is a positive, neutral of negative description. Ask them to check with the
other pair and, if necessary suggest alternative adjectives to help the description.

Follow up

- Ask the students to take the role of their famous person and write an e-mail describing
themselves to a stranger meeting them at an airport. Emphasise that they should be more
positive about themselves and not describe their personality!

- Tell the students to write an e-mail to a company enquiring about a job vacancy. In it they
should give a positive description of their personality and why they are interested in the job.

Ways of Describing People

Adjectives: describing bodyshape

Positive	Neutral	Negative
a .... slim **c**	overweight thin muscular	fat **b** .... muscle-bound

Adjectives: describing personality

Positive	Neutral	Negative
d .... clear-sighted self-contained	persuasive confident quiet	bullying **e** .... **f** ....

Put these adjectives in the correct boxes: shy skinny plump forceful beefy arrogant

E-mail 1

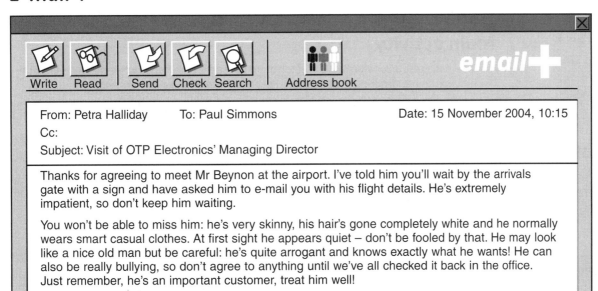

From: Petra Halliday   To: Paul Simmons   Date: 15 November 2004, 10:15
Cc:
Subject: Visit of OTP Electronics' Managing Director

Thanks for agreeing to meet Mr Beynon at the airport. I've told him you'll wait by the arrivals gate with a sign and have asked him to e-mail you with his flight details. He's extremely impatient, so don't keep him waiting.

You won't be able to miss him: he's very skinny, his hair's gone completely white and he normally wears smart casual clothes. At first sight he appears quiet – don't be fooled by that. He may look like a nice old man but be careful: he's quite arrogant and knows exactly what he wants! He can also be really bullying, so don't agree to anything until we've all checked it back in the office. Just remember, he's an important customer, treat him well!

E-mail 2

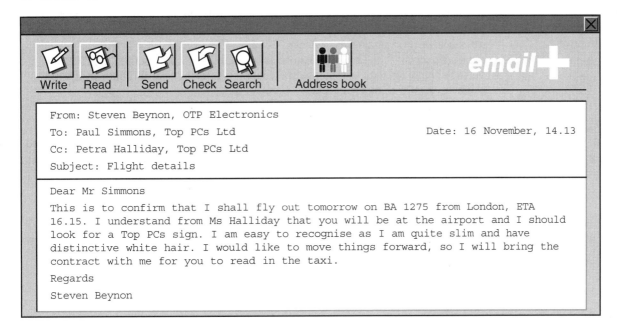

From: Steven Beynon, OTP Electronics
To: Paul Simmons, Top PCs Ltd   Date: 16 November, 14.13
Cc: Petra Halliday, Top PCs Ltd
Subject: Flight details

Dear Mr Simmons
This is to confirm that I shall fly out tomorrow on BA 1275 from London, ETA 16.15. I understand from Ms Halliday that you will be at the airport and I should look for a Top PCs sign. I am easy to recognise as I am quite slim and have distinctive white hair. I would like to move things forward, so I will bring the contract with me for you to read in the taxi.

Regards

Steven Beynon

8.3

LEVEL
Upper-intermediate

TOPIC
Introducing
characters

ACTIVITY TYPE
Text analysis

**WRITING
FOCUS**
Fiction

TIME
50 minutes

KEY LANGUAGE
*agile, broad, capable,
deft, delicate, discreet,
fine-boned, flesh, furry,
knuckles, narrator,
palm, protecting,
slender, squat, tanned,
threatening, veins, wrist*

PREPARATION:
One photocopy, cut up,
for each pair of
students; monolingual
dictionaries; enough
pictures of different,
unknown people to
give one to each pair
of students (see Main
activity, step 4)

The shape of hands ...

Warm up

1   In pairs, give each pair a copy of Part 1. Give them five minutes to look at the pictures and match the Adjectives of physical description to the different hands, 1–3. If they do not know some of the adjectives, encourage them to look them up in dictionaries.

> **Suggested answer**
> **1** a, b, h   **2** c, d, e, f, g   **3** a, b

2   Brainstorm which Adjectives of character the students feel might be used to describe the owners of each set of hands. Emphasise that this is subjective.

> **Suggested answer**
> **1** j, k, l, n   **2** m, n   **3** k, l

Main activity

1   Give each pair a copy of Part 2 and tell them to read it and match a pair of hands from the pictures to the description in the text. Feedback as a whole class. (Answer: 2)

2   Explain that the narrator is Harry's wife. Ask the students to read the description again and answer the Analysing Meaning questions in their pairs. Feedback as a whole class.

> **Suggested answer**
> **a**   4, 6, 7
> **b**   1, 2, 3, 5, 8, 9, 10, 11
> **c**   Something has happened that means she can only think of him in a fragmented way.
> **d**   This is subjective, but probably not.

Ask the students to look at the text again and answer the Analysing Style questions.

> **Suggested answer**
> **e**   Longer than twelve words
> **f**   Twelve words or shorter (Elicit how the grammar breaks up in 8, 9, 10 and 11, reinforcing the narrator's view of Harry.)
> **g**   Something has happened to the hands and they no longer do these things.
> **h**   1, 3, 4, 5 (Elicit how the negative clauses are foregrounded in the early sentences to make the reader aware there is a problem with the narrator's relationship with Harry.)

3   Elicit how the reader does not know Harry's job or history but through the description of his hands they do have a sense of who he is and how he relates to the narrator.

4   Give each pair one of the pictures you have brought with you. Tell them to look carefully at the picture and discuss the person's character and how that person would react in these situations: being in a train crash; winning €1,000,000; a woman giving birth in their car. Tell the pairs to think of one physical feature or piece of clothing that summarises that person's character. Explain that they should write a brief fictional introduction for that character, similar to that in Part 2.

5   Join the pairs into groups of six. Tell them to read their descriptions out loud while the others in the group take notes on how they see/understand the person's character. The writers should then discuss with the others if they have given the impression they wanted to. Tell the group to discuss which description worked best and why.

6   Ask the pairs to redraft their descriptions, taking into account what has been said in the group.

Follow up

●   Ask the students to swap pictures. Ask them to think of a critical situation, similar to those in step 4. Tell them to write a story about how the character they wrote about in the lesson and the person in the new picture react in the critical situation.

●   Tell the students that their character wants to apply for a job. Tell them to write the application letter explaining who they are and why they are applying.

Part 1

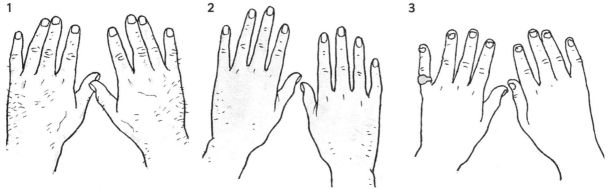

Adjectives of physical description:

a short **b** broad **c** tanned **d** slender **e** deft **f** delicate **g** fine-boned **h** furry **i** agile

Adjectives of character:

j protecting **k** threatening **l** powerful **m** discreet **n** capable

---

Part 2

[1]I don't see him whole, only bits and pieces. [2]And of those bits and pieces, his hands most clearly. [3]I cannot imagine having married a different shape of hands. [4]Never the short, squat, broad, fur-knuckled kind that one pictures oily from say, engine parts, crude and threatening. [5]Not that Harry's hands lacked power, but it was another sort. [6]Long slender fingers, deft and agile, never clumsy, attached to the fine bones of his hand, tanned flesh over blue veins, colours that blend delicately and well. [7]And ending at the wrists, the prominent, sticking-out bones of the wrists, a dusting of pale hair. [8]Discreet hands. [9]Protecting and capable hands. [10]Hands that knew and saw and did. [11]Hands that would know me and take care.

From *Dancing in the Dark* by Joan Barfoot, the Women's Press, 1982

Analysing Meaning

a Which sentences describe hands?

b Which sentences describe the narrator's thoughts and opinions?

c What do you think the narrator means when she says she does not see Harry whole?

d Do you think the narrator has a good relationship with Harry? Why, or why not?

Analysing Style

e How long are the sentences that describe hands?

f How long are the sentences that describe the narrator's thoughts and opinions?

g Why does the narrator use the simple past tense in sentence 10?

h Underline the negative clauses. Where do they occur? Why?

9.1

LEVEL
Elementary

TOPIC
Personal belongings

ACTIVITY TYPE
Whole class game

WRITING FOCUS
Catalogue descriptions

TIME
50 minutes

KEY LANGUAGE
auction, bid, cheap, expensive, huge, leather, medium-priced, metal, plastic, wood, tiny;
Order of adjectives

PREPARATION
For the Warm up: if possible, arrange that you and your students each bring a treasured possession. Alternatively, you can easily use everyday objects. Hide your possession in a bag. One photocopy, cut up, for each group of four students

Note: If you are unfamiliar with Internet auctions, try visiting www.ebay.co.uk

Internet bargains

Warm up

Prepare by placing something in your bag. Tell the class they must guess what is in your bag. Explain that it is something important to you but do not say what it is. Elicit what questions they could ask and write these on the board: *Where is it from? What is it made of? What colour is it? How big is it? How expensive is it? Why is it important to you?* As students ask these questions, write the answers on the board, eliciting *It's + adjective.* Ensure you leave the questions on the board.

Main activity

1   In groups of four, give each group a set of Mix 'n' Match Cards. Ask the students to put the question cards in a row, A-E. They must then take it in turns to choose an adjective card and put it under the correct question. Do the first one with them as an example. Feedback as a whole class. **Note:** Both C and B are correct for *gold.*

2   Give each group a copy of the descriptions and ask the students to rearrange the Mix 'n' Match Cards so that they copy the Descriptions. Emphasise that they will not use all the adjectives. Demonstrate the first sentence on the board: *An (E) expensive (D) small (C) white (A) French (B) leather handbag.* Feedback as a whole class and elicit the order in which the Mix 'n' Match questions are answered in descriptions: *a/an ... (E) value (D) size/age (C) colour (A) origin (B) material ... thing.*

3   In pairs, ask them to show each other the special thing they have brought with them and work together to write the descriptions. Tell them they must describe what each item is and why people will want to buy it. Explain they can create an imaginary history for the objects to make them more attractive to a buyer.

4   In groups of four, ask them to swap their descriptions and check them for accuracy.

5   Explain that they are going to take part in an Internet auction. Their descriptions will be displayed on a 'website', i.e. the classroom notice boards, and people will make 'secret' offers for the items. Tell them to select the description of their most saleable item and pass it to you. Collect and number the descriptions and display them around the room.

6   Explain they have €100 to spend and all bids are secret. Give each group a colour as a code-name. Tell them to read the descriptions and write the number of those items that interest them. When they have sat down again, give each group four Bid Cards. Tell them to decide what they are going to bid for and how much they will bid.

7   Collect the cards and award the items to the highest bidders!

Follow up

●   Ask the students to write the description of something they own, omitting the noun. Get them to swap the descriptions and guess what the things are.

●   Ask the students to write a letter to a friend describing the amazing bargain they got on the Internet.

Mix 'n' Match Cards

A Where is it from? It's …	B What is it made of? It's …	C What colour is it? It's …	D How big is it? It's …	E How expensive is it? It's …
French	wood	blue	tiny	free
Swiss	metal	gold	small	cheap
Japanese	plastic	white	big	medium-priced
Swedish	leather	black	huge	expensive

Descriptions

1 It's an expensive small white French leather handbag. The President gave it to me in 2000.
2 It's a huge Scandinavian wood desk. It shows you are the boss!
3 It's a tiny black Japanese plastic translator. It was the first ever made.
4 It's a medium-priced Swiss gold watch. I bought it in the Grand Bazaar in Istanbul.

Bid Cards

INTERNET AUCTION BID CARD	
Item:	
Group's Colour:	
Bid:	

INTERNET AUCTION BID CARD	
Item:	
Group's Colour:	
Bid:	

INTERNET AUCTION BID CARD	
Item:	
Group's Colour:	
Bid:	

INTERNET AUCTION BID CARD	
Item:	
Group's Colour:	
Bid:	

9.2

It's a whatsit

LEVEL
Intermediate

TOPIC
Everyday objects

ACTIVITY TYPE
Group quiz

WRITING FOCUS
Dictionary definitions

TIME
50 minutes

KEY LANGUAGE
corkscrew, device, dresser, machine, saucer, tool, twisted;

Defining relative clauses; *(used) to* + infinitive ... / *for* verb+*ing* ...

PREPARATION
One photocopy of the Mind Map and Whole Class Quiz Clues and pictures, cut up, for each pair of students; one photocopy, cut up, of Group 1 and Group 2 Quiz Clues and pictures for each four students; one set of Picture Cues, cut up, for each 20 students

Note: Students can complete the definitions they have written to those in a real dictionary by visiting http://dictionary.cambridge.org

Warm up

1 Tell the students you have completely lost your memory. Pick up a pen and elicit what it is and its function. Write on the board: *It's a thing which you use for writing.*

2 Put the students in pairs and give out one copy of the Mind Map for each pair. Elicit how it groups things from top to bottom, from the general to the specific. Ask the students to add two more machines/devices and tools to the lists and complete the definitions.

3 After three minutes ask them to check their answers with another pair. Feedback as a whole class.

> **Answer key**
> 3 A hammer is a tool for hitting nails.
> 5 An office is a place where business people work.

Main activity

1 Give each pair one copy of the Whole Class Quiz Clue for a dresser, without the picture. Read it through as a whole class, checking difficult vocabulary. Give the pairs one minute, without dictionaries, to decide which is the correct definition.

2 After one minute, write a, b and c on the board. Tell the students to raise their hands for the definition they think is correct and write the total number of students who think each definition is correct under the corresponding letter.

3 Give each pair a copy of the picture of the dresser. Feedback which is the correct definition.

> **Answer key**
> a (b = a dressing; c = a mannequin)

4 Divide the class into two groups, 1 and 2. Give each group enough copies of the corresponding Quiz Clue, without the picture, so that students have one copy between two. Tell them to discuss the clues in their groups and decide which is the correct definition. After five minutes give out the Quiz Clue pictures and feedback.

> **Answer key**
> **Group 1:** b (a = a screwdriver; c = a corker)
> **Group 2:** c (a = a wizard / sorcerer; b = a saucepan)

5 As a whole class, brainstorm the structures used in the definitions. Write this on the board:

A specific noun is a general noun | *with / consisting of* ... parts
(used) to+infinitive ... /*for* verb+*ing* ...
which/that/who/where ...

Elicit how the descriptions can be linked together, e.g. in the description of the saucepan.

6 Put the students in pairs and show each pair a different Picture Cue. Tell them to think of two words that are similar to the name of the object but not write them down. If they can't think of two similar real English words, ask them to invent them! Ask them to write down definitions for all three words.

7 When the students have had sufficient time, ask them to join another pair as a group of four and swap definitions. Ask them to check that the other pairs' definitions can be understood and are accurate English. Tell them to feedback to each other and then redraft their own definitions.

8 Explain to each group of four that they are a team. Ask them to join another team and swap their definitions. Tell the teams to decide which are the correct definitions. When they have had sufficient time, they should check their answers together.

Follow up

● Ask the students to compile a dictionary for tourists. It must contain words for things which appear only in your country or region of the world.

● Ask the students to imagine a new invention, give it a name and write the dictionary definition for it.

Mind Map

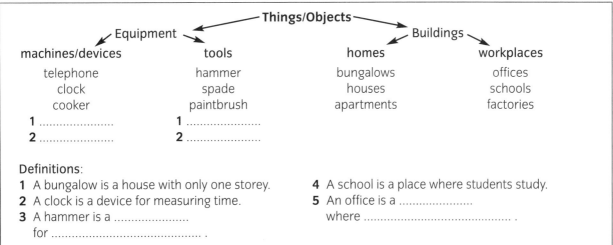

Things/Objects

Equipment → machines/devices, tools
Buildings → homes, workplaces

machines/devices	tools	homes	workplaces
telephone	hammer	bungalows	offices
clock	spade	houses	schools
cooker	paintbrush	apartments	factories

1 ....   1 ....

2 ....   2 ....

Definitions:
1 A bungalow is a house with only one storey.
2 A clock is a device for measuring time.
3 A hammer is a ....
  for ....

4 A school is a place where students study.
5 An office is a ....
  where ....

Quiz Clues

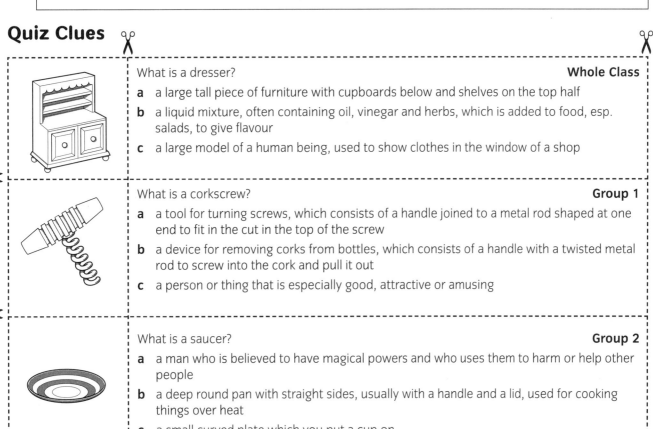

What is a dresser? **Whole Class**
a a large tall piece of furniture with cupboards below and shelves on the top half
b a liquid mixture, often containing oil, vinegar and herbs, which is added to food, esp. salads, to give flavour
c a large model of a human being, used to show clothes in the window of a shop

What is a corkscrew? **Group 1**
a a tool for turning screws, which consists of a handle joined to a metal rod shaped at one end to fit in the cut in the top of the screw
b a device for removing corks from bottles, which consists of a handle with a twisted metal rod to screw into the cork and pull it out
c a person or thing that is especially good, attractive or amusing

What is a saucer? **Group 2**
a a man who is believed to have magical powers and who uses them to harm or help other people
b a deep round pan with straight sides, usually with a handle and a lid, used for cooking things over heat
c a small curved plate which you put a cup on

Picture Cues

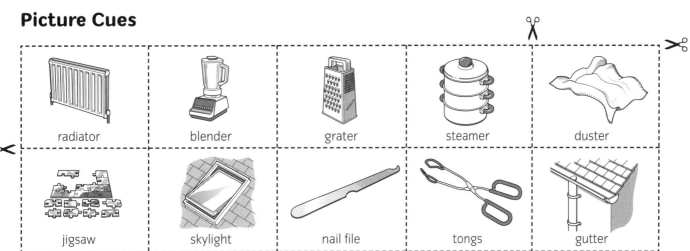

radiator	blender	grater	steamer	duster
jigsaw	skylight	nail file	tongs	gutter

9.3

Dream limo

LEVEL
Upper-intermediate

TOPIC
Custom limousines

ACTIVITY TYPE
Paired simulation

WRITING FOCUS
Fax; checking for meaning

TIME
50 minutes

KEY LANGUAGE
to customise something, external, mood lighting, passenger compartment, removable top, specifications, stretch limo, trim; vocabulary of description

PREPARATION
One photocopy, cut up, for each pair of students

Optionally, one photocopy of Writing style 2 (p.126) for each student

Warm up

1 Quickly brainstorm everything that students associate with stretch limousines, e.g. Hollywood, luxury, stars, etc.

2 Ask them to decide what they would include in their dream limo – tell them to be as creative as possible! As the students answer write notes on the board for future reference.

Main activity

1 In pairs, give each pair a copy of the advertisement. Tell them to read it and discuss how similar the limo is to their dream limo. Elicit the meaning of difficult vocabulary from context, e.g. *trim, removable top, passenger compartment, mood lighting,* etc.

2 As a whole class brainstorm possible alternative options to those given. As you do this, categorise those already on the board.

> **Suggested answer**
> **Make:** Lincoln or Jaguar S-type; **Size:** 20m (seats 6) / 30m (seats 8) / 40m (seats 10) / 50m (seats 12) 60m (seats 14); **Colour:** Black or white; **External trim:** Gold or chrome; fixed roof or removable top; **Passenger compartment specifications:** Bar or coffee station; music centre or DVD player; TV and video player or satellite TV; leather or artificial fur seats; dining table or computer workstation; mood lighting or disco lighting

3 In pairs, tell the students to choose one option in each category and write a list of their own personal specifications. They can also add any other categories and options they want.

4 Give each pair a copy of the Fax. Elicit who sent it, what it's about and the level of formality. Give them one minute to find formal expressions in the fax which mean: 1 asked about; 2 buying; 3 agree; 4 as soon as possible.

> **Answer key**
> 1 expressed an interest in
> 2 purchasing
> 3 confirm
> 4 at the earliest possible opportunity

5 Elicit the conventions of the layout of faxes, i.e. the subject line, CC, etc.

6 Explain that this fax has been sent to the students regarding their custom limo. In pairs, tell them to write a reply which follows the conventions. Brainstorm formal words and phrases that the students are likely to use in their reply, e.g. *With reference to ..., I was disappointed to find ..., Please amend the specifications ...,* etc. You may want to give the students a copy of Writing style 2 to help with this (see p.126). In their reply they must say what Dream Limos has got wrong, i.e. anything that differs from the list they made for step 3. Tell them they want the car to be perfect. To ensure this they must be precise in their description of what to include, e.g. *a black leather J-shaped seat.*

7 After ten minutes, tell the pairs to swap their fax with another pair. Explain that they are now sales people for Dream Limos. Explain that they cannot start work until they are sure they understand the specifications. Tell them to read the new fax and write questions against anything that could be misunderstood, e.g. *Which side of the car do you want the black leather J-shaped seat on?*

8 After ten minutes, tell the students to swap back their faxes and redraft them so that all the questions are answered.

Follow up

- Tell the students to write a fax to a motor company ordering a custom-made family car. They should specify exactly what they would like included in the car.

- Tell the students to write a magazine advertisement for their limo or family car.

Advertisement

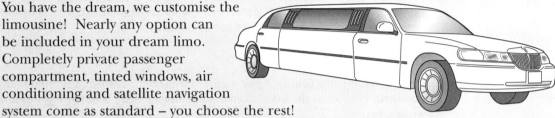

DREAM LIMOS

Lincoln (30m) White with gold trim and a removable top for cruising in the sun. The luxurious passenger compartment includes a black leather J-shaped seat for up to eight people, a light wood coffee station and dining table, satellite TV and mood lighting for that special occasion.

You have the dream, we customise the limousine! Nearly any option can be included in your dream limo. Completely private passenger compartment, tinted windows, air conditioning and satellite navigation system come as standard – you choose the rest!

Fax

FACSIMILE TRANSMITTAL SHEET	

TO: New Customer	**FROM:** Sales, Dream Limos
FAX: 044 223 245361	**PAGES:** 1 of 1
PHONE: 044 223 245382	**DATE:** 28 August 2004
RE: Your custom limo	**CC:** Workshop, Dream Limos

☐ URGENT ☑ FOR REVIEW ☐ PLEASE COMMENT ☑ PLEASE REPLY

Thank you for your recent telephone call in which you expressed an interest in purchasing one of our custom limousines. We would be grateful if you could confirm that the specifications you require are as follows:

Make: Jaguar, S-type   **Size:** 20m
Colour: Black   **External Trim:** chrome
Roof: fixed

Passenger compartment specifications: Dark wood coffee station; DVD; satellite TV; artificial fur seats; computer workstation; disco lighting

We shall look forward to receiving your confirmation, so that we can start work at the earliest possible opportunity.

10.1

LEVEL
Elementary

TOPIC
Crisis in a
relationship

ACTIVITY TYPE
Paired role play

**WRITING
FOCUS**
Personal letter
(giving news)

TIME
50 minutes

KEY LANGUAGE
*to cheat, to change
your mind, fees, to
finish with someone,
to let someone know
(something) to take
care of (something);*
Explaining and
apologising; past and
future tenses

PREPARATION
One photocopy, cut up,
for each pair of
students

Dear John …

Warm up

1   Draw this picture on the board and elicit what has happened.

Explain: *I've met a man. I'm in love.* Ask: *Do I tell my
friends by phone or write?* (Phone – it's quicker.)

2   Put a cross over the heart and elicit what has happened:

Explain: *I don't love my boyfriend now.* Ask: *I want to finish
with him. Do I phone him or write?* (Write – it's more final.)

3   Write: *Dear John…* Elicit who John is (your boyfriend) and what you might say in the letter.
Explain that this kind of letter is known as a 'Dear John letter'. Discuss if it is true that good
news comes by phone and bad news comes by letter.

Main activity

1   Put the class in pairs. Give each pair a copy of the Letter. Tell them they must answer these
questions: *Who wrote the letter? Who is he writing to? Why is he writing?* Feedback as a
whole class.

> **Answer key**
> Richard – a student
> His parents
> He's been asked to leave university for cheating: he wants to explain and come home.

Explain that Richard tries to make the news less upsetting by using 'softening' phrases, i.e.
The thing is … / Well … / You see … Elicit phrases that he uses to apologise, i.e. *I'm afraid …
/ I'm really sorry …* and highlight how he uses *will* to suggest a way of improving things,
i.e. *I'll get a job.*

2   Put the students in two groups, 1 and 2, and give each group copies of their numbered
role card. Explain that there are two situations on each role card. Ask them to read the
cards and check any difficult vocabulary.

3   In their groups, tell them to discuss each situation, who they would write to and what they
would say.

4   Divide each group into pairs and tell them to choose one of the situations from their role
card and write the letter. Explain that they can adapt the photocopied Letter as a first draft
by writing directly onto it. They can choose to keep phrases, add to them and cross out or
change anything that is not relevant.

5   Ask each pair to join with a pair from the same group and swap letters. Tell them to
answer these questions: *Do I understand what the writer is saying? Can I make it clearer?*
Explain they must redraft it on a new piece of paper.

6   Ask each pair to join with a pair from a different group and swap letters. Ask them to read
the new letter in their pairs and answer the same questions you asked for the
photocopied Letter (see step 1 above).

7   Ask them to check their answers with the writers of the letter.

Follow up

•   Ask the students to take the role of the person who has received the letter. Ask: *How does
this message make you feel? What will you do next?* Tell them to write a reply.

•   Ask them to write the letter they would most like to receive.

Letter

Brent Valley University

1 June 2004

Dear Mum and Dad

I hope everything's okay with you. I'm afraid things aren't too good with me. I don't know how to tell you this but ...

Well, last week someone saw me reading a note in my final exam. It was only something to help me remember. You see, they think I was cheating. It's crazy!

The thing is, they want me to leave the university. I'm still talking to them. I hope they'll change their minds but I don't think they will.

I'm really sorry. I was stupid. I know you'll be very disappointed. I'll get a job to pay you back the fees, I promise! Please don't be too upset.

Love

Richard

Role Cards

Group 1

a   Your brother is working in a different country for a year. He loves his pet dog, Rex. You are taking care of Rex while he's away. Two days ago Rex ran away from you and you don't know where he is now.

b   Your sister is away at university. Yesterday, you went to a nightclub with her boyfriend. You were enjoying yourself and you kissed him. Now he says he wants to finish with her, he loves you and he's going to tell her that. You don't love him.

Group 2

a   You borrowed your best friend's watch without telling them. It was a present from their boyfriend/girlfriend. You dropped it and it broke.

b   When you first met your university friends you wanted them to like you. You told them your parents were very rich. It's not true! Your house is very small and now your friends want to visit you.

10.2

LEVEL
Intermediate

TOPIC
New soap opera
characters

ACTIVITY TYPE
Paired simulation

**WRITING
FOCUS**
Feature article;
expanding ideas

TIME
50 minutes

KEY LANGUAGE
*to get on with
(someone), nickname,
optimist, outgoing,
pessimist,
relationships, shy,
situations*

PREPARATION
One photocopy, cut up,
for each pair of
students

Soap opera

Warm up

1 Elicit what a soap opera is, i.e. a long-running TV/radio series about a set group of characters which you can see/listen to at least once every week. Brainstorm the names of popular soap operas that the students know.

2 Write these headings on the board: *Stories; Characters; Locations;* and elicit what is similar about the soap operas that the students have brainstormed.

> **Suggested answer**
> **Stories:** relationship problems, illness, etc.; different storylines are used in the same programme / continue over several programmes; each programme finishes with a crisis
> **Characters:** stereotypes, e.g. the reliable friend, the villain, etc.; characters from a wide range of age-groups
> **Locations:** generally domestic and at least one location where lots of characters can meet, e.g. pub, café, workplace, etc.

Main activity

1 Brainstorm a title and main location for a new soap opera and write it on the board. Put the students in pairs and give each pair a blank Character Template. Explain that they have five minutes to think of a character for the soap opera. Ask them to use their imaginations to complete sections 1–4 of the Character Template.

2 After five minutes tell the pairs to join together with another pair. Explain that the characters they have described on their templates belong to the same family. Ask them to swap their template with the other pair and read about the other pair's character. In their group of four, ask them to discuss how the two characters will relate to each other and whether there should be any other characters in the family. After five minutes ask them to swap back templates and complete section 5, continuing on the back of the paper if necessary.

3 In their groups, ask the students to make notes on: *the best location for introducing the family; an event that shows how the characters in the family relate to each other.*

4 Give the students the Feature Article. Explain it comes from a TV listings magazine and is about an episode which introduces a new family into a soap opera. Ask them to read it and check any difficult vocabulary, e.g. *rowdy, to give up, squabbling, turns up, a housewarming do,* etc. Elicit what the new family is like and how the last sentence makes the reader want to watch the programme to find out what has happened to Ruth.

5 Split the groups into their pairs again and ask them to write a similar article about the episode that introduces their character's family.

6 After ten minutes, ask the students to join with the other pair they worked with previously and swap articles. Ask them to read the article and then compare it with their own. As a group of four, ask them to decide which article best describes the family and which would make them want to watch the programme.

Follow up

- Tell the students to write a short biography of one of the characters in the family for the soap's website.

- Tell the students they represent the TV company. Tell them they want to make the soap opera appeal to a different audience, i.e. younger or older. Tell them to write a memo giving details of a proposed new family that will appeal to the new audience.

Character Template

1	Name:		Nickname:	
	Age:	Weight and Height:	Job:	
	Education:		Hobbies:	
	Poor/Middle income/Rich	Optimist/Pessimist	Shy/Outgoing	
2	What situations make them feel comfortable or uncomfortable?			
3	What do they want to do with their life?			
4	What have they done in the past that they are embarrassed about?			
5	Who are their family? How do they get on with them?			

Feature Article

WHAT'S ON

Meet the Gordons

Rowdy new family the Gordons move into the Close this week.

Dad Alan is having a hard time trying to give up smoking, while his three teenage children are squabbling over rooms.

On top of that, the first neighbour he meets is Ron Dixon, who turns up to complain about the noise from their unofficial housewarming do.

However, Alan has bigger problems to deal with when his eldest daughter Ruth, appears, covered in bruises.

From *tvchoice*, 29 June 2002

10.3

Who gets the children?

LEVEL
Upper-intermediate

TOPIC
Pre-nuptial
agreements

ACTIVITY TYPE
Paired role play,
text analysis

**WRITING
FOCUS**
Formal contract;
adding punctuation

TIME
50 minutes

KEY LANGUAGE
*alimony, assets,
contract, to drop a
hint, expenses,
fiancée, ground rules,
to have a hold over
somebody, income,
legal parties,
pre-nuptial, retain,
sleazy, to throw
a party*

PREPARATION
One photocopy, cut up,
for each pair of
students

Optionally, one
photocopy of Writing
style 1 (p.125) for
each student

Warm up

1 Write this list on the board: *age, physical appearance, character, interests, money, family background*. Tell the students to rank these qualities from 1 to 6 (1 = most important, 6 = least important) in choosing someone to marry.

2 In pairs, tell students to discuss why they ranked the qualities the way they have. Feedback as a whole class.

Main activity

1 Divide the class into two groups, A and B. Tell group A they are a rock star called Mark Bragger and group B that they are his fiancée, Mandy Pauper. Explain that they want to make a formal pre-nuptial agreement before their marriage. Elicit what types of thing might be included, e.g. who gets what property or money if they ever split up.

2 Give each student a copy of the appropriate Role Card and tell them to discuss in their groups what they would put in a formal agreement before the marriage.

3 Give each student a copy of the Pre-nuptial Agreement. Ask them to check it contains what they wanted to include and to punctuate it. Feedback as a whole class.

> **Suggested answer**
> This agreement is made on 2 January 2006 between Mark Bragger of Brash Hall, Hertfordshire, England and Mandy Pauper of 12 Victoria Road, Ealing, England.
> Whereas
> Mark and Mandy are to be married on 3 August 2006 at Saint Mary's Church, Hanwell, England.
> The parties agree as follows:
> 1 Mark and Mandy shall share all income and expenses equally.
> 2 Each party shall be responsible for any expenses they bring to the marriage.
> 3 Each party shall remain the owner of any assets they bring to the marriage.
> 4 If Mark and Mandy divorce, each shall retain the assets they brought to the relationship. In addition, they will equally share any income or expenses since their wedding.
> Signed .... Signed ....
> Date ....

4 Elicit examples of the formal style used, e.g. the passive in the first sentence, the use of *shall* instead of *will* and *party* instead of *person*, etc. Explain that in general English *whereas* usually means *in contrast to* or *by comparison with*. In this example of legal English it is similar to *since* as it introduces a statement followed by a list and shows the list can only be true if the statement is true.

5 Pair the students, one from each group. Tell them to discuss, in role, their concerns and to draw up an additional section of the agreement to cover matters such as children, careers, duties within the marriage, etc. Tell them to be as clear as possible, to never say they will reach agreement about something at a later date, and to have realistic expectations! Emphasise they have only ten minutes and must reach agreement.

6 After ten minutes, tell the pairs to swap their contract with another pair and check it for anything that might be misunderstood and for style. You may want to give students a copy of Writing style 1 to help them with this (see p.125).

7 Tell the pairs to join together and discuss how the agreements should be redrafted.

Follow up

- Ask the students to choose two real companies that do or make similar things. Explain that the companies are going to merge. Ask the students to write the contract.

- Tell the students to write a formal letter to a lawyer asking them to check the agreement.

Role Cards

✂

(Group A)

Mark Bragger, 54

You are the millionaire lead singer of *Ageing Bones*. You have already had two wives and do not want to lose any more money in alimony through another failed marriage. Your first wife travelled on tour with the group and constantly got in the way, especially when you were trying to practise. At one time, the group nearly split up because of her. Your second wife was a top model. She had big arguments with your housekeeper, Estelle, who used to be your childhood nanny and has always been a second mother to you.

Recently, you have started to feel your age. You want a quieter life and children to play with! You have been going out with Mandy Pauper for six months and feel it is time to marry again. You first met Mandy at a party your record company was throwing. You think she has the most amazing smile. Most attractive women try to catch your eye but Mandy ignored you. You could not resist the challenge.

✂

(Group B)

Mandy Pauper, 22

You are a journalist with great prospects. It was your editor who suggested you might get an interview with the 54 year old rocker, Mark Bragger, by making contact at his record company's party. You thought Mark was sleazy but he is really very romantic. You have been going out with him for six months now. You have read his biographies and know about his past wives and his long-term housekeeper, Estelle. Estelle is very possessive: she seems to have a hold over Mark which you do not like.

Recently, Mark has been dropping big hints about marriage and you want to set a few ground rules. After all, he is so much older than you ... he might just want your body! You want time and freedom to make a name for yourself as a travel writer. It will mean a lot of hard work but Mark will also be on tour for a lot of the time. You definitely do not want to have children until you are in your thirties.

✂ -

Pre-nuptial Agreement

Regarding property and finances:

this agreement is made on 2 january 2006 between mark bragger of brash hall hertfordshire england and mandy pauper of 12 victoria road ealing england

whereas

mark and mandy are to be married on 3 august 2006 at saint marys church hanwell england

the parties agree as follows

1 mark and mandy shall share all income and expenses equally

2 each party shall be responsible for any expenses they bring to the marriage

3 each party shall remain the owner of any assets they bring to the marriage

4 if mark and mandy divorce each shall retain the assets they brought to the relationship in addition they will equally share any income or expenses since their wedding

signed .... signed .... date ....

11.1

More gain, less pain

LEVEL
Elementary

TOPIC
Encouraging healthy lifestyles

ACTIVITY TYPE
Group text analysis

WRITING FOCUS
Website feature article; expanding ideas

TIME
50 minutes

KEY LANGUAGE
advice, to encourage, exercise, to be fit/unfit, gain, to get fit, hard work, to keep fit, keeping fit, to keep on (doing something), kids, to overdo something, pain;
Giving advice (*should, could,* etc.)

PREPARATION
Two photocopies for each group of four students: cut up one for each group and leave the other one whole

Warm up

1 Divide the class into two groups, 1 and 2. Mime dancing or draw on the board someone dancing, and ask them to guess what you are doing/drawing. Award a point to the group that guesses first. Ask a student to come to the front, and to mime or draw on the board the activity you tell them. Whisper to the student: *skateboarding*. Repeat for *jogging, cycling, soccer, walking a dog, ice-skating,* and *weight-lifting*. Total the points!

2 Ask what these activities have in common, i.e. they are ways of doing exercise and keeping fit. Elicit the difference between *to get fit*, i.e. become fit, *to be fit/unfit,* and *to keep fit*, i.e. stay fit. Write on the board: *There's no gain without pain*. Discuss what it means and if they think exercise has to be painful to do any good.

Main activity

1 Put the students in groups of four. Give out one copy of the top part of the Web page, including Section 1, to each group. Explain that it is part of a web page about keeping fit. Ask them to decide, as a group, what kind of people visit the website. Feedback as a whole class. (Answer: Parents who think their children are unfit.)

2 Ask the groups to reread Section 1 and find the three pieces of advice. Feedback as a whole class.

> **Answer key**
> Do exercise yourself; Do exercise every day; Walk instead of driving

3 Elicit how the structure of the section reinforces the message, i.e. a statement (*Show your kids …*), then advice (*You should …*), and then a positive possibility (*You could …*) .

4 Give out one copy of the remaining sections of the cut-up Web page per group. Tell them to read the headers of each section and decide as a group what each might be about. Feedback as a whole class.

> **Suggested answer**
> 2 encouraging small children
> 3 encouraging people to be sensible about how much exercise to do
> 4 showing people that keeping fit is fun
> 5 encouraging teenagers to keep fit

5 Divide each group in half and tell the pairs to take two of the sections each and think of three pieces of advice to include in each. Tell the students to discuss their answers in their group. Feedback as a whole class.

> **Suggested answer**
> 2 play outside / kick a ball about / learn to cycle
> 3 don't do too much / 1 hour a day / 20 minutes' hard exercise
> 4 get a dog / try a sport with your friends / try dancing, skateboarding, etc.
> 5 be independent: cycle! / learn to dance! / meet friends at sports clubs

6 Tell the pairs to write in complete sentences on both sections of the Web page. When they have finished, tell them to swap with the other pair in their group, read the new sections and check they understand the advice given.

7 Give out one copy of the Web page per group. In groups tell them to combine their sections into one Web page, checking for accuracy as they redraft the Web page.

Follow up

● Ask the students to redesign their keep fit page so that it appeals to either 5–10-year-olds or 15-year-olds.

● Ask the students to rewrite their keep fit page as a 100-word article for a teenage magazine.

Web Page

| Beauty | Kids | FAQs |

More gain, less pain ...
... encourage your kids to keep fit

1 Mum and Dad – get fit!

Show your kids how to do it – if they see you enjoying exercise, they're more likely to enjoy it themselves. You should spend time every day keeping fit: jogging, exercising in front of the TV ... anything! And you shouldn't drive, walk: on those small shopping trips, leave the car at home and cycle or walk the 100 metres to the shop. You could even take the kids with you!

2 Little kids – keeping fit starts early ...

3 Don't overdo it!

4 It's not all hard work!

5 Teenagers: keep on keeping fit

BYE DAD!

11.2

First Aid

LEVEL
Intermediate

TOPIC
Emergency First Aid

ACTIVITY TYPE
Paired text analysis,
simulation

WRITING FOCUS
Informative leaflet;
editing for logic
and focus

TIME
50 minutes

KEY LANGUAGE
*advice, bent, burn,
cloth, injured, injury,
ointment, plasters,
sling, to support
(something), to swell,
to tie something (tight);*
If + present tenses

PREPARATION
One photocopy, cut up,
for each pair of
students; one
photocopy of the
Second draft checklist
(p.120) for each pair of
students

Note: You can get
more information on
First Aid by visiting
www.bbc.co.uk/health

Warm up

Mime walking across the front of the room and falling onto a desk. Pretend you have broken your arm. Elicit what you have done Ask: *What should I do now?* Brainstorm notes onto the board and elicit the vocabulary items *pain, an injury, to support (the arm)* and *a sling*. As an alternative to mime, draw an arm in a sling on the board to elicit the vocabulary.

Main activity

1 Explain to the students that they are going to read part of a First Aid leaflet for parents of young children. In pairs, give each pair a cut-up copy of the Advice on Broken Arms. Tell them to arrange it in the most logical order.

2 After five minutes, feedback as a whole class and discuss any difficult vocabulary. Elicit why the text uses bullet points, clear simple instructions and pictures, i.e. for quick reference by people who are panicking.

3 Write on the board: *I've burnt myself.* Elicit what this means. Brainstorm what you should do with a burn. Explain that you are going to give the students unfinished notes about burns from the same leaflet. The information has been prioritised but the text still needs to be edited.

4 In pairs, give each pair a copy of Advice on Burns. Refer them to the pictures, and ask them to read the advice and edit the text, linking or cutting points, so that there is only one bullet point for each picture and each bullet point is clear and easy to understand.

5 After ten minutes, ask them to swap their advice with another pair. Ask them to read the new advice, underline anything that needs to be made clearer and cross out anything that they think can be cut.

6 After five minutes, tell them to join with the other pair, swap back their advice and check if they agree with the corrections.

7 Give each pair a copy of the Second draft checklist. Ask them to read it and use it to correct their own advice.

8 If there is time, put the pairs of students in groups of six. Ask them to swap their three advice sheets with another group. Tell them to read the new advice sheets and select the clearest. One person should then feedback to the other group.

> **Suggested answer**
> - Take or cut off watches and clothes immediately. If any clothes are burnt onto the skin, leave them for a doctor to remove.
> - Hold the burn under cold running water for at least ten minutes.
> - Do not use ointment or plasters. If you do, it is difficult for the doctor to see the burn.
> - Cover the burn with a clean cloth. Tie another cloth loosely around it as a bandage.
> - If the burn is small, you still need to see a doctor. Any burn can be dangerous to a child.

Follow up

- Tell the students to write similar advice about what to do with cuts.

- Explain that the First Aid leaflet they have worked on will be left in doctors' surgeries, libraries, schools, etc., for people to pick up. It will have four pages: a front cover, one page about broken bones, one about burns and one about cuts. The students must design the front cover. Explain that it must be eye-catching and they must decide what information to include on the cover.

Advice on Broken Arms

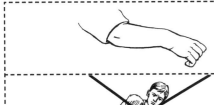
- If there is pain or swelling or the arm looks bent, it may be broken.

- Do not move the injured child unless absolutely necessary. Call a doctor.

- If a doctor cannot come, take the child to hospital. Make sure the broken arm is well supported.

- If the arm will bend easily, use a sling and tie cloth around the arm and chest to hold it in place.

- If the arm will not bend, put some cloth between the body and arm and tie three pieces of cloth around the arm and body.

Advice on Burns

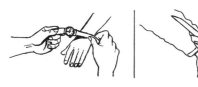 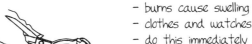
- burns cause swelling
- clothes and watches can get tight and hurt you
- do this immediately
- only doctors should remove anything that is burnt onto the skin

- cold water helps
- do this immediately
- use a tap
- do this for 10 minutes or more

 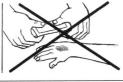
- plasters do not help
- ointment can make burns worse
- doctors can't see a burn with a plaster on it

- use clean cloth on the burn
- use more cloth as a bandage
- do not tie it very tight

- small burns can be dangerous to children
- children should see a doctor immediately

The Donor Campaign

LEVEL
Upper-intermediate

TOPIC
Organ donor
campaign

ACTIVITY TYPE
Group simulation

**WRITING
FOCUS**
TV advert
storyboard

TIME
50 minutes

KEY LANGUAGE
Body parts: *corneas
(eyes), kidneys, heart,
liver, lungs, pancreas,
small bowel, bone, skin*;
*to donate, donation,
donor, medical condition
sound effects (SFX)
transplants, to transplant,
voice-over (VO)*

PREPARATION
One photocopy, cut up, for
each pair of students

Note: Get more information
on organ donation by visiting
linked sites at
www.uktransplant.org.uk

To view real blood donation
TV adverts visit
www.blood.co.uk

Warm up

1   Ask if anyone has ever donated blood and why they did it. Brainstorm what other organs and tissues can be donated and the vocabulary *a transplant, to transplant* and *donor*.

> **Suggested answer**
> heart, kidneys, corneas (eyes), lungs, pancreas, small bowel, liver, bone and skin

2   Ask: *How many people in the world have had a transplant? Can old people be donors? What are skin donations used for?* Give each pair a copy of Organ Donor Facts. Tell them to check their answers and discuss anything that surprised them. Feedback as a whole class.

Main activity

1   Tell the students that people are dying who could be saved with a transplant. They have been given the job of creating a 30-second TV advertisement that will encourage more people to donate their organs for transplant.

2   In groups of four, tell them they have five minutes to discuss these questions:
At what time of day will the advert be broadcast, between what kind of programmes? How do you want to make the viewer feel? e.g. scared, guilty, positive, etc. How are you going to persuade the viewer to respond immediately? How is the viewer going to respond? e.g. phone, write a letter, contact a website, etc.

3   After five minutes, ask the groups to split into two pairs. Explain that they are two separate creative teams working for the same advertising agency in competition. Give each pair a copy of the Storyboard template. Explain that they are going to prepare a rough outline of their advertisement to present to the organ donor organisation before filming. Elicit the vocabulary *a voice-over,* i.e. someone speaking while the camera is filming something else, and *sound effects* (abbreviated to *VO* and *SFX*). Tell the pairs at this stage not to write on the templates. Explain they have five minutes to discuss and decide on the rough outline of their advert.

4   After five minutes ask the pairs to summarise their advertisement by writing notes describing what happens in the three ten-second segments – the opening, middle and close – on the storyboard. Ask them also to write a separate bulleted list giving the reasoning behind the choices they have made.

5   After ten minutes, tell the pairs to regroup into their groups of four. Explain that the advertising agency will present both adverts to the organ donor organisation, who will select one to be made. Put two groups of four together, and ask one group to present their two adverts and the reasons behind them to the other four. The other four should select one to be made and feedback the reasons for their selection. After ten minutes, reverse the roles and ask the second group to present their adverts and the first group to select one.

Follow up

●   Ask the students to design and write the campaign's poster or magazine advert.

●   Ask the students to decide on a major star they want to appear in their TV advert. Tell them to write a letter to the star explaining why they should act in it for a minimal fee.

Organ Donor Facts

1 Over one million people world-wide have had a transplant in the last 25 years.

2 Medical advances mean more people nowadays can be helped by a transplant.

3 There are not enough donors to match the number of patients waiting for a transplant.

4 There is no maximum age for some donations.

5 If a potential donor has a medical condition they can still sometimes donate organs.

6 Donation of corneas helps to restore sight, heart valves to treat heart disease and skin to treat burns.

✂ --

Storyboard

	Opening – 10 secs	Middle Segment – 10 secs	Close – 10 secs
Visual i.e. what the viewer can see			
Speech/VO/ SFX i.e. what is said or the viewer can hear			
Action i.e. what happens			
Text i.e. what is written on the screen			

12.1

Leisure for all

LEVEL
Elementary

TOPIC
Planning a
sports/leisure centre

ACTIVITY TYPE
Group simulation

**WRITING
FOCUS**
Questionnaire

TIME
50 minutes

KEY LANGUAGE
Vocabulary of sport:
*alley, court, gym, pitch,
pool, rink*; *facility,
leisure, local*;

Open and closed
questions

PREPARATION
One photocopy, cut up,
for each student

Warm up

1 Give out one copy of the Sports Puzzle to each student and explain that they should complete the puzzle, using the seven sports illustrated. Feedback as a whole class.

> **Answer key**
> **1** bowling   **2** ice-skating   **3** swimming   **4** basketball   **5** tennis   **6** football
> **7** weight-training

Explain that you *play basketball/football/tennis* (sports for more than one person) but *go swimming/ice-skating/bowling/weight-training* (sports that you can do on your own).

2 Brainstorm five other sports.

Main activity

1 Tell the students that you work for the local government of a small town called Royston. You plan to build a new sports/leisure centre. Write on the board: *What information do we need before we build the leisure centre?* Brainstorm as a whole class.

> **Suggested answer**
> What sports facilities are already available.
> What local people want.

2 Put the students in groups of four and give out one copy of the Profile to each student. Ask: *Can you go swimming in Royston? No; Can you go weight-training? Yes; How far away is the nearest indoor tennis court? 1–15 km away.* Highlight the vocabulary for specific sporting facilities, e.g. *court, pool,* etc. Tell the groups to discuss what facilities they think Royston needs.

3 As a whole class, explain that the local government has asked them to write a questionnaire to find out what the people want. Explain that they already know what facilities are available locally so they are unlikely to use *can* (for ability) questions in their questionnaire. Brainstorm what questions might be useful. Accept all suggestions and write them on the board.

4 Give out one copy of the Sports Questions for each student. Ask them to write answers to the questions. After five minutes, feedback as a whole class. Elicit the different responses for closed *Do …, Yes/No* and open *How/Wh …* questions and demonstrate how each elicits different types of information.

5 In groups of four, tell the students to write the questionnaire. Explain they must decide on the best mix of closed and open questions. Tell them to either select ten from the board or write ten new ones and put them in a logical order.

6 Tell the groups to test their questionnaire on another group to ensure it gathers all the information they need.

Follow up

- Tell the students that a TV company wants to create a new TV channel in their town or region. The company wants to find out what people watch already, e.g. news, soap operas, drama, sport, etc. and what they would like to watch on the new channel. Ask the students to write a questionnaire that the company can give to the public.

- Ask the students to choose a sport or leisure activity which they like. They must write a letter to the local government saying why it is important that the new sports/leisure centre should include facilities for that sport or activity.

Sports Puzzle

Clues

1
2
3
4
5
6
7

---✂--

Profile: Royston is a small town near Cambridge, England. 15,000 people live in Royston.

Where can I find these facilities?	Basketball court	Swimming pool	Football pitch	Ice-skating rink	Bowling alley	Indoor tennis court	Weight-training gym
In town	No	No	Yes	No	No	No	Yes
1–15 km away	No	Yes	Yes	No	No	Yes	Yes

---✂--

Sports Questions

1 What sports do you play?

....

2 Do you play football?

....

3 How often do you go swimming?

....

4 Do you go ice-skating every week?

....

12.2

I win!

LEVEL
Intermediate

TOPIC
Explaining board games

ACTIVITY TYPE
Group board game

WRITING FOCUS
Instructions, rules

TIME
50 minutes

KEY LANGUAGE
aim, board, connected/unconnected, diagonal, to lose, move, object, opponent, piece, player, row, rules, to take a piece, to take a turn, the winner;

When/If ..., ... can ... (zero conditional)

PREPARATION
One photocopy, cut up, of the Nine Men's Morris Board and Pieces for each group of four students; one photocopy of the Nine Men's Morris Rules for each pair of students

Warm up

1 Put the class into groups of four and give each group a copy of the Nine Men's Morris Board. Brainstorm what it is, i.e. a board for a game called Nine Men's Morris. Ask if anyone has played it and quickly elicit the names of other board games and general board game vocabulary, e.g. *to win/lose, a piece, your opponent,* etc.

2 Give each group two copies of Nine Men's Morris rules. Tell them to read them quickly and find two nouns that link to the verb *to take.* (Answer: *a piece, a turn.*) Elicit the difference between *to move a piece* and *to take a piece* (*off the board*).

Main activity

1 As a whole class, brainstorm how the rules are structured and elicit headings for each section, i.e. the aim/object (1–4); how to play and win (5–8); the stages of the game (9–16). Elicit where to put extra spacing or line breaks in the text to make it easier to understand, i.e. after 4, 8, 11 and 14.

2 Tell the students to check they understand the rules in their groups. Give one student in each group the black pieces and another student the white pieces. Explain that they are going to play the game while the other two members of the group observe, check if they are following the rules and advise them on the best moves. After ten minutes stop the games.

3 Write Stage 2 of the rules on the board and elicit the difference in meaning between the *When* and *If* conditionals. Tell the students to underline examples in other sections. Feedback as a whole class and elicit other characteristics of the text, e.g. conciseness, use of the present simple and non-use of subject pronouns.

4 In their groups, tell students they have ten minutes to write the rules of another game. Ensure the groups do not hear the name of the others' games. Tell half the groups to write the rules for Battleships (Salvo) and tell the other half to write the rules for Draughts (Checkers). If these games are unfamiliar to your students, use two of the simpler games which they brainstormed in the Warm up. Tell them to use the structure of the Nine Men's Morris Rules as a model. They should not write the name of the game on their rules!

5 After ten minutes, ask the groups to swap their rules with a group from the other half of the class. Ask them to try to guess what game is being described.

6 Ask the students to check with the other group what the game is and redraft the rules to make the structure clearer and the rules easier to understand.

Follow up

● Ask the students to write the instructions for Noughts and Crosses (Tic Tac Toe), or another traditional board game.

● Ask the students to think of a task which they do regularly at home or work, e.g. switching on a computer and starting up a word processing programme. Tell the students that they have had an accident and until they are better someone will have to do the task for them. Ask them to write instructions to help that person with the task.

Nine Men's Morris Board and Pieces

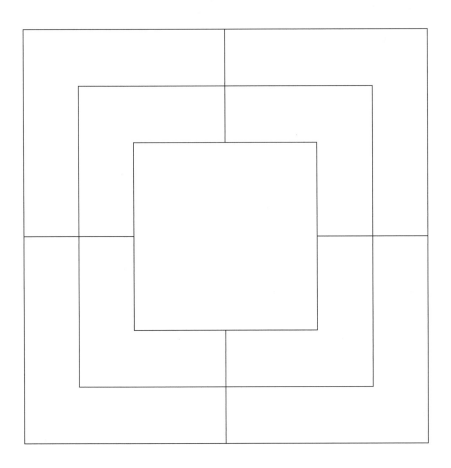

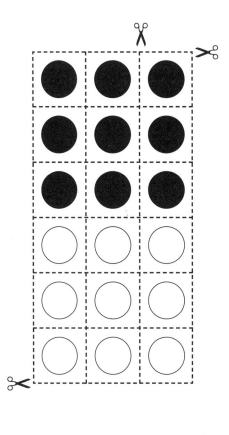

Nine Men's Morris Rules

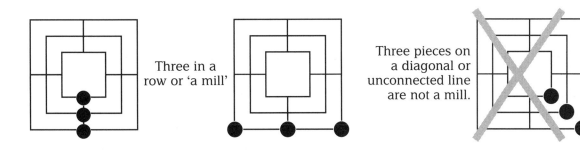

Three in a row or 'a mill'

Three pieces on a diagonal or unconnected line are not a mill.

[1] There are two players. [2] Each player has nine pieces, or 'men'. [3] The object of the game is to trap your opponent so they can no longer move, or to capture seven of their playing pieces. [4] Each player must try to do this by putting three pieces in a row or 'mill' on a connected line. [5] The game has three stages. [6] In Stage 1, the player who makes a mill can move one of their opponent's pieces. [7] In Stage 2 and 3, the player who makes a mill can take away one of their opponent's pieces. [8] The winner is the person who takes seven of the other player's pieces. [9] **Stage 1:** At the start of the game the board is empty. [10] Each player takes it in turns to put a piece on any point on the board where two lines connect. [11] If a player makes a mill, they can move one of the other player's pieces to another point on the board. [12] **Stage 2:** When all the pieces have been put on the board, each player moves a piece along a line to an empty point. [13] They can only move one space at a time, and not diagonally. [14] If a player makes a mill, they can take one of the other player's pieces off the board. [15] **Stage 3:** When a player has only three pieces left, they can jump one piece to any empty point on the board. [16] A player who has only two pieces left, or who cannot move any of their pieces, loses the game.

A really good read ...

LEVEL
Upper-intermediate

TOPIC
Reviewing for a website

ACTIVITY TYPE
Paired text analysis

WRITING FOCUS
reviews; correcting style and structure

TIME
50 minutes

KEY LANGUAGE
bullying, catchy, emotive, genre, immortal, nerd, orphan, qualify, riveting, to shower somebody (with something), theme, wizard

PREPARATION
One photocopy, cut up, for each pair of students; one photocopy of the First draft checklist (p.120) for each pair of students

Note: If you have an OHP, you may want to make an OHT of the photocopiable page to use in step 3

You can download more reviews for this target audience from www.readingmatters.co.uk

Warm up

Brainstorm the titles of books and films the students have read or seen recently. Discuss how the students heard about the books or films and why they chose to read or see them. Discuss how much a good or bad review would influence their choice.

Main activity

1 Tell the students that they are going to rewrite a brief review of the book *Harry Potter and the Philosopher's Stone* for a children's / young person's website. Explain that it has been written badly and the site's editor has returned it to be redrafted. Briefly brainstorm what might be wrong with it.

2 In pairs, give each pair a copy of the Draft Review. Ask them to read it and check their predictions, marking on it where they think there are weaknesses in the review. After ten minutes, give each pair a copy of the First draft checklist. As a whole class, elicit what comments and error codes the editor might put on the review and where.

3 Give each pair a copy of the Editor's Comments and ask them to decide if they agree with the comments. As a whole class, brainstorm the revisions to the review.

4 Ask: *What should be included in a book or film review?* Draw this blank table on the board, without the entries in italics. Refer to your revision as you brainstorm the points in italics.

Contents	*Structure*
1 Your opinion	*1 Books: title/author/publisher*
2 Facts:	*Films: title/classification/director/ stars*
– main theme of book or film, i.e. what happens (plot), who it happens to (characters), and where it happens (setting)	*2 Catchy introduction*
	3 Brief factual paragraph
– genre, e.g. horror, romance, adventure, etc.	*4 Paragraph stating your opinion*
– writer's style, e.g. factual, literary, emotive, etc.	*5 Catchy conclusion/recommendation which refers back to the introduction*
Review style: Active not passive verbs; no repetition; no qualifying your opinions	

Elicit how the type of target audience will also affect the choice of style, i.e. as this is for a young person's website it uses a conversational, informal style and short words but a review in an arts magazine might use a more formal style.

5 Ask the students to choose a book or film they know and review it for either the young person's website or an arts magazine.

6 If there is time, ask the students to swap their reviews, read the new review and act as editor by annotating it using the First draft checklist.

Follow up

● Ask the students to rewrite their review for a different target audience, e.g. a lifestyle magazine for older people (60+).

● Ask the students to each find a different magazine and read any reviews it contains. Explain that the magazine gets sent many reviews that are unsuitable. The editor has asked them to write some brief notes on reviewing to help potential contributors. These must include notes on what is normally reviewed in the magazine, how long the reviews are and the writing style that is used.

Draft Review

Review	Editor's Comments

Review

Harry Potter and the Philosopher's Stone
J. K. Rowling (Bloomsbury Publishing)

Harry Potter is an orphan who lives with his Uncle Vernon, Aunt Petunia and their bullying son, Dudley. He doesn't know he's a wizard.

I think the struggle between good and evil, between death and life, has always fascinated young people, and in Rowling's capable hands makes a riveting read for adults too. In my opinion, the book does not rely only on its excellent plot: Rowling's prose is carefully crafted, she builds suspense well and tells a good joke too.

Harry, the 'nerd', is forced to live in a cupboard under the stairs and thinks his parents were killed in a car crash. But then he is spoken to by a snake, showered with letters by owls and whisked away from his suburban nightmare to Hogwarts School of Witchcraft and Wizardry. In this magical school, where pictures are doors and staircases move, he learns he is the only one who can fight Voldemort and he is unique: the only survivor in an attack by the evil wizard Voldemort which killed his parents. He discovers his destiny is to save the Philosopher's Stone before Voldemort finds it and becomes immortal. In doing so, he nearly dies himself.

Although not yet a literary classic, *Harry Potter and the Philosopher's Stone* is a really good read. It forces you to ask questions about good and evil and might even stop you hiding in your own cupboard under the stairs.

Editor's Comments

Start   Boring! Catch the reader.

St   Use adjectives: *miserable orphan, dreadful* bullying son, etc.

/   It is fascinating or it isn't. Not ~~I think, In my opinion,~~ etc.

2 ⟩   Swap the paragraphs. Tell me about the book before you tell me about the genre and Rowling's style.

1 ↙

 St   Use the active, not the passive.

Rep   Don't repeat yourself.

/   Don't tell me how the book ends.

End   Nice ending – link it to the beginning.

13.1

A likely excuse ...

LEVEL
Elementary

TOPIC
Excuses for absence

ACTIVITY TYPE
Group board game

WRITING FOCUS
Absence note

TIME
50 minutes

KEY LANGUAGE
absence, to miss (something), nurse, schedule, timetable;

I'm very sorry / Please forgive me for (not) verb+ing; I couldn't ... because ...

PREPARATION
One photocopy, cut up, of the Example for each pair of students; one photocopy of the Excuses Game Board and two Game Pieces for each group of four students

Optionally, one simplified photocopy of the Second draft checklist (p.120) for each student

Warm up

1 Brainstorm reasons why students might miss a lesson. Write on the board: *I couldn't come because ... I had to go to hospital.* Put the students in groups of four and tell them to write four more possible excuses.

2 Feedback as a whole class and write the excuses on the board. Ask them to rank the excuses according to how believable they are (0 = unbelievable, 5 = believable).

Main activity

1 Put the students in pairs and give each pair one copy of the completed Example. Explain that the excuse is for a famous fictional character who they must guess. Feedback as a whole class. (Answer: Shakespeare's Juliet)

2 Ask: *Why is Juliet sorry? Why wasn't she in school yesterday? What is she going to do?*

> **Answer key**
> Because she was not in school yesterday.
> She went to see a nurse.
> She is going to do the work she missed at home.

As you feedback, write this table on the board, eliciting how the note is structured:

> **Apology:** *I'm very sorry for (not)* verb+*ing / Please forgive me for (not)* verb+*ing*
>
> **Explanation:** *I didn't / I couldn't ... because ...*
>
> **Promise to do something:** *I'll ...*

3 In their pairs, ask the students to use the table to write either two excuse notes to their teacher or two notes giving excuses for missing business appointments, on separate pieces of paper. The excuses should be as believable as possible.

4 Join the pairs into groups of four. Give each group one copy of the Excuses Game Board and two Game Pieces. Tell them this is either their school timetable or work schedule, and ask them to write one subject or appointment in each of the eight slots, e.g. *Maths* or *Meeting with Mrs Planer.*

5 Tell the students this is a race to get to home time.

Rules of the game
- Tell each pair in the group to choose a Game Piece and put it on the Timetable/Schedule slot.
- Show the students a coin and explain that the head side is worth two moves and the reverse side is worth one. Ask each group to flip a coin to see which pair goes first. The first pair should move either one or two spaces, according to the flip of the coin.
- If Pair 1 lands on ☹ they must give Pair 2 their written excuse. Pair 2 must decide if the excuse is believable and discuss it with Pair 1. If it is believable, Pair 1 leaves its Game Piece where it is. If it is unacceptable, they move back one space.
- If a pair lands on Lunch they take another go.
- If a pair lands on ☹ and has used both their excuses, they must invent a new one.
- The first pair to get to Home time is the winner.

6 At the end of the game, tell the pairs to re-read their opponents' excuses and check them for language errors. You may wish to give students a simplified copy of the Second draft checklist to help them with this (see p.120).

Follow up
- Ask the students to choose one of these situations and write an excuse: you forgot your mother's birthday; you missed your brother's wedding; you forgot to meet an important customer at the airport.
- Ask the students to choose another fictional character and, in role, write their excuse note. Later ask the students to swap excuses and guess which fictional character wrote the note.

Excuses Game Board

Timetable/Schedule

1	8.00
2	9.00
3	10.00
4	11.00
5	12.00
Lunch	
6	14.00
7	15.00
8	16.00
Home time	

Example

23 via Cappello
Verona
Veneto

21 April 1594

Dear Teacher

I'm very sorry for not coming to school yesterday. I didn't come because I drank something bad and had to see a nurse quickly. I'm afraid Romeo is also going to be away for a long time. In fact we may not see him at school again.

Please give me any work I missed yesterday. I'll make sure I do it!

Yours faithfully

J----- Capulet

Game Pieces

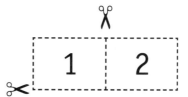

13.2

LEVEL
Intermediate

TOPIC
The writing process

ACTIVITY TYPE
Paired simulation

WRITING FOCUS
Promotional flier; targeting audience

TIME
50 minutes

KEY LANGUAGE
college prospectus, communicate, course, draft, edit, form (genre), flier;

Present simple;
will + infinitive

PREPARATION
One photocopy, cut up, for each pair of students; one photocopy of the First draft checklist (p.120) for each pair of students; one photocopy of the Second draft checklist (p.120) for each pair of students

Writing class

Warm up

1   In pairs, give each pair a copy of the College Prospectus. Brainstorm what it is and why you might read it.

2   Tell them someone wants to get more information about the course and she has written a letter. Give each pair a set of the Writer's Notes. Explain that the four drafts show different stages in writing the letter, and the two thought bubbles show the writer's thoughts. Ask the pairs to put the six items in the correct order.

Answer key
e, a, c, b, d, f

Main activity

1   While the students are doing the Warm up, draw this flow chart on the board, omitting the arrows, answers in italics and asterisks (*).

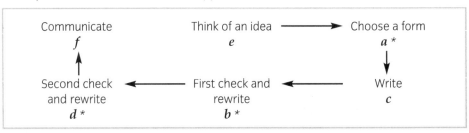

2   As a whole class, brainstorm the correct heading on the chart for each of the six items. Elicit where the flow chart starts and finishes and add the arrows.

3   Elicit other things that might go under the asterisked (*) headings, e.g. Choose a form – personal letter, note, e-mail, diary, novel; First check and rewrite – checking for meaning and formality, moving paragraphs, cutting / adding; Second check and rewrite – checking punctuation, spelling and grammar.

4   Explain to the students that the college needs to attract more people to the writing course. They have a limited budget. Elicit ways of doing this, e.g. a short promotional flier. Elicit the characteristics of a flier, i.e. no more than one side of A5; it will include a visually attractive headline, concise information and contact details. Highlight how they have thought of an idea (*e*) and chosen a form (*a*). Explain that they are going to continue with the process and, in pairs, write the flier. They should make the course appear relevant and exciting. If they want to, they can use the information in the Prospectus as a basis for their leaflet.

5   After ten minutes, ask each pair to swap their flier with another pair. Ask them to read the new flier and decide whether it would persuade them to join the course. Give each pair a copy of the First draft checklist and tell them to use the code to mark any areas where the flier could be improved.

6   After five minutes, ask the pairs to swap their fliers back and feedback to each other. Ask them to redraft their own flier to make it clearer and more appealing.

7   If there is time, give each pair a copy of the Second draft checklist and ask them to use it to check their draft for technical and grammatical errors.

Follow up

●   Ask the students to write a similar leaflet promoting a music course.

●   Ask the students to write their own letter applying for a place on an educational course.

College Prospectus

Writing Extra   Tutor: Mr T Winton

In this evening course students will learn the basics of writing. The course examines the process of drafting, editing and writing a finished piece. Students will learn to write e-mails, letters, reports, fiction and much more.

✂ -

Writer's Notes

e

I want to improve my writing.

a

I need to write a letter and ask for information.

c

Dear College, I want

to improve my

writing.

Love P.

Send informations

about your course.

b

Dear Sir or Madam

i want to improve

my writing.

Yours faithfully

Ms P. Sims

Send informations

about your course.

d

Dear Sir or Madam

i would like to improve

my writing.

Please send ^informations

about your course.

Yours faithfully

Ms P. Sims

f

21 Hills Road
Southampton
SH3 7BD

13 September 2004

Dear Sir or Madam
I would like to improve
my writing.
Please send some information
about your course.
Yours faithfully
Ms P. Sims

13.3

LEVEL
Upper-intermediate

TOPIC
Virtual language
schools

ACTIVITY TYPE
Group discussion,
text analysis

**WRITING
FOCUS**
discursive
composition; linking
ideas

TIME
50 minutes

KEY LANGUAGE
*factor, generate, ideal,
the next best thing,
pros and cons,
virtual language
school;*
Discourse markers

PREPARATION
One photocopy for
each student
Note: You may wish to
visit
www.selfaccess.com or
www.englishtown.com
to see how a virtual
language school works

Cyberstudy

Warm up

1 If you are not studying in an English-speaking country, ask if anyone has been to an English-speaking country to study English. Ask what it was like and how useful it was.

2 Brainstorm what a 'virtual language school' is, whether anyone has used one on the Internet and what differences there might be between virtual schools and more traditional ones. In groups of four, ask the students to list the pros (positive points) and cons (negative points) of each form of learning, e.g. accessibility, cost, native-speaker pronunciation teachers, etc. Feedback as a whole class.

Main activity

1 Write on the board: *'The virtual language school – not language travel – is now the best way to learn English.' To what extent do you agree or disagree with this statement?*

2 In their groups, tell the students to make notes on what they would include in the composition and prioritise their notes.

3 Give each student a copy of the Model Composition and ask them to read it and discuss in their groups whether they agree with the writer or not and why. After five minutes, feedback as a whole class.

4 Tell the students to match the discourse markers in italics in the text with those in the boxes. Show how (1) has been done as an example. **Note:** some can be used in more than one box. Feedback as a whole class.

> **Answer key**
> **a** 6   **b** 8   **c** 2   **d** 4   **e** 3   **f** 10   **g/h** 5, 9   **i** 7

5 Elicit how these discourse markers are words or phrases that highlight the writer's attitude and emphasise the logical connections within the text. Demonstrate the use of commas after many of the discourse markers, and point out how *still* and *however* both link a positive and negative sentence, but *while* and *whereas* link positive and negative clauses and are put at the front of a sentence, e.g.
Learning with a teacher is preferable. Still/However, it is not essential for everybody.
Whereas/While this is preferable, it is not essential for everybody.

Elicit other sequencing discourse markers, e.g. *secondly, thirdly,* etc.

6 Ask the students to plan their own composition, using their notes from step 2. Explain that they do not have to write a finished composition but have five minutes to write a plan in note form.

7 After five minutes, put the students in pairs. Ask them to explain the logic of their composition plans to each other and discuss which discourse markers they could use to indicate the flow of ideas and opinions.

8 After five minutes, ask the students to expand their plan into a 200-word essay using appropriate discourse markers. If there is sufficient time at the end of the lesson, ask them to swap the first draft of their composition with their partner and give their partner's composition a mark out of ten for the clarity of its organisation.

Follow up

● Ask the students to write a 180-word composition with this title: *'Education is wasted on some people. Discuss.'*

● Ask the students to write an advertisement for a virtual school for a magazine for young people.

Model Composition

'The virtual language school – not language travel – is now the best way to learn English. Discuss.'

[1] *In my opinion*, studying English in countries where it is the first language will always be the ideal. [2] *However*, many factors always have to be taken into account when choosing a language course.

[3] *Firstly*, there is cost. [4] *While* travelling to experience the language in its home environment is always preferable, it is expensive both in terms of time and money. [5] *As a result*, more and more people have turned to virtual internet schools which are accessible from a computer anywhere in the world at anytime of the day. [6] *In addition*, virtual schools now employ native-speakers who offer online pronunciation practice and conversation classes.

Secondly, there is the place where you learn. [7] *In general*, a 'real' classroom with real people will always generate more communication than a computer screen and keyboard ever could. [8] *Similarly*, a virtual school can never provide those important extras such as a study centre or close contact with an English-speaking homestay family. [9] *In consequence*, they will never replace the real thing.

[10] *To sum up*, virtual language schools are a useful alternative to, but not a replacement for, traditional English language courses in English-speaking countries. For those who do not have the time or money to travel, they are the next best thing.

Match the discourse markers from the text with similar markers in each box:

Linked ideas that agree	
a	Besides,
b	In the same way,

Linked ideas that do not agree	
c	Still,
d	Whereas (+), (-)

Ideas in a sequence	
e (i.e. *1*, 2, 3)	Lastly, (i.e. 1, 2, *3*)
f	In conclusion,

One idea is the logical result of another	
g	So
h	Consequently,

Opinions	
On the whole,	i
As I see it,	j (1) In my opinion

14.1

Trouble with telesales

LEVEL
Elementary

TOPIC
Business problems

ACTIVITY TYPE
Group simulation

WRITING FOCUS
Memo; using capital letters

TIME
50 minutes

KEY LANGUAGE
aggressive, company, complaint, insurance, to lie, Managing Director, memo/memorandum, to sell (something), telesales

PREPARATION
One photocopy, cut up, for each pair of students

Note: for more information on writing memos visit www.managementhelp. org/writing/memosmpl.htm

Warm up

1   Write on the board: *What am I doing? What is my job?* Pretend to dial a telephone number and say *'Hello, is that Mrs Smith? You don't know me but my company can help you ...'* Elicit that you are a telephone sales person, and explain that *telephone sales* is normally abbreviated to *telesales*. Ask if any of the students have worked in telesales and elicit why they like or dislike telephone sales people.

2   In pairs, give each pair a copy of the Memo. Explain that the telephone sales department at SL Insurance has got problems and the Managing Director is worried.

3   Ask the students: *What are the two most important problems for the company?* Feedback as a whole class.

> **Answer key**
> Customers have complained about dishonest sales people.
> The company is not selling enough.

Main activity

1   In pairs, ask the students to reread the Memo and complete the exercise.

> **Answer key**
> **a** 5   **b** 3   **c** 2   **d** 1   **e** 4   **f** 6

2   Explain that when Martin Finch wrote the Memo, the shift key on his computer got stuck and so there are no capital letters. Ask the students, in their pairs, to underline every letter that should be a capital. Feedback as a whole class, eliciting how all names, e.g. *Amanda, January* and titles, e.g. *Managing Director* should have a capital letter. Elicit how the prompts, i.e. *to, from, date* and *re* should start with a capital letter but each item on the list should not because they continue the sentence *Customers say:*.

3   Elicit how a memo does not have the greeting *Dear ...* or the closing formula *Best wishes ...* that you might expect in a letter or e-mail, and how it is concise and to the point.

4   Draw a smiley face on the board: ☺. Explain that each pair has its own company. Ask: *What is your company called? What does it make or sell?* Draw a sad face on the board: ☹. Ask: *What are your company's problems?*

5   Ask the pairs to write a memo, similar to the model memo, from the Managing Director of their company explaining the problems to an employee and asking for a response. Ask them only to write on alternate lines on their paper.

6   When the students have had enough time, ask them to swap their memo with another pair. Ask them to check that they understand the problems and write a question mark by anything they do not understand.

7   Ask the pairs to underline any mistakes or anything that should have a capital letter.

8   Ask the students to swap back their memos and correct them. Give each pair a copy of the Memo Template to write their final version on. They should continue on the back if they run out of space.

Follow up

●   Explain that Amanda has been encouraging her sales people to improve sales. Ask the students to write her reply to the Managing Director. Explain that it must be positive and answer all the Managing Director's points.

●   Ask the students to write the memo that they would most like to receive.

Model Memo

Memorandum

SL Insurance
'We care for you'

to: ¹ amanda bennett, head of telesales
         cc personnel department

from: ² martin finch, managing director   date: 20 september 2004

³ re: complaints

⁴ we are receiving far too many complaints about our telephone sales people. customers say:

⁵ • our sales people lie about other insurance companies and try to steal their customers;

• our sales people promise good things but do not help if there is a problem;

• our sales people are aggressive on the phone.

it is not surprising that the company is not selling much. ⁶ i want to know before tomorrow what you are going to do about it.

Where are these things? Match each lettered item to a number in the memo:

a   a list ....

b   a word that tells you what the memo is about (an abbreviation of *with regard to*) ....

c   the person who wrote the memo ....

d   the person who the memo is to ....

e   words that explain why the memo was written ....

f   words that explain what the writer wants ....

✂ ---

Memo Template

Memorandum

To:

From: Date:

Re:

14.2

What do you do?

LEVEL
Intermediate

TOPIC
Describing and managing work

ACTIVITY TYPE
Paired text analysis, guessing game

WRITING FOCUS
Job description

TIME
50 minutes

KEY LANGUAGE
to advise, to develop, extension, fridge, Line Manager, to manage, to monitor, to operate, Practice Nurse, to produce, responsibilities, to swipe, syringes, vaccines

PREPARATION
One photocopy, cut up, of the 'To Do' Lists a and b and Sample Job Descriptions for each pair of students; one photocopy, cut up, of 'To Do' Lists c and d for each four students

Optionally, one photocopy of Writing style 1 (p.125) for each student

Warm up

1 Brainstorm what a *'to do' list* is, i.e. a list of tasks that a particular person needs or wants to get done in the near future. As a whole class, brainstorm what would appear on a student's 'to do' list.

2 In pairs, give each pair a copy of 'To Do' Lists a and b and tell them to guess the people's jobs. Feedback as a whole class. (Answer: **a** Supermarket Checkout Operator, **b** Librarian)

Main activity

1 Give each pair a copy of the Sample Job Descriptions. Explain that they describe the jobs for 'To Do' Lists a and b. Tell them to match them to the 'To Do' Lists and complete the job titles. (Answer: **1**b, **2**a)

2 Tell them to complete the job titles of the Line Managers. (Answer: **1** Supervisor, **2** Chief Librarian) Feedback as a whole class and check difficult vocabulary.

3 Brainstorm the characteristics of a job description, i.e. three-part structure which clearly differentiates responsibilities (general, particular, additional); tasks are prioritised; concise bullet points; simple sentence structure (implied subject+transitive verb+object+phrase, e.g. *monitors the cash in the till*); use of present simple; use of formal verbs specific to the job, not general verbs.

4 Write this table on the board and tell the students to link each general verb to a specific verb. All the specific verbs are used in the Sample Job Descriptions.

Similar verbs	
General / less formal ——————→	**Specific / more formal**
check	advise
fill	monitor
organise	pack
change	develop
help	manage
use	collect
take	operate

Feedback as a whole class.

> **Answer key**
> check → monitor; fill → pack; organise → manage; change → develop;
> help → advise; use → operate; take → collect

5 Split the class into two groups. Give one group enough copies of 'To Do' List c for one copy per pair; give the other group enough copies of 'To Do' List d for one copy per pair. Explain that each group has a different 'To Do' List and that they must keep their job a secret from the other group. Ensure that you do not accidentally reveal their secret while helping with vocabulary! Ask the pairs to write at least one more 'to do' item on their list.

6 After three minutes, tell the pairs to redraft and expand the list into a job description. Emphasise that they must prioritise the responsibilities and, wherever possible, use specific verbs. Tell them to ensure that they do not include the job title. Emphasise that they should use more specific/formal alternatives to the verbs in the 'To Do' Lists, e.g. *meet with* (not *see*), *construct* (not *build*), *contact* (not *phone*), *purchase* (not *buy*), etc. You may want to give students a copy of Writing style 1 to help them with this (see p.125).

7 After ten minutes, tell the pairs to swap the job description with a pair from the other group and guess the job title. Tell them to feedback to the other pair and discuss if they agree with the way the responsibilities are prioritised and the choice of verbs.

Follow up

• Ask the students to interview someone they know about their job, and write their job description.

• Ask the students to write a letter to apply for a job discussed in the lesson.

'To Do' Lists

a

To do

- find out the price of tomatoes
- get more £5 notes for the till
- ask supervisor for new chair!
- check where pasta's been moved

b

To do

- check if Mrs Preece's book has arrived and phone her
- send off inter-library loans
- contact Chief Librarian about faulty light

✂--

✂

c Practice Nurse's 'To do' list

- phone hospital about blood tests
- check vaccines in the fridge
- check syringes
- see and help patients

d Builder's 'To do' list

- phone architect about plans for extension
- get bricks
- phone electrician to fit lights
- build extension

✂-- ✂

Sample Job Descriptions

Job description 1

Job title:

General responsibilities
Responsible for the operation of a library.

Main responsibilities
- *checks in / out books, tapes, CDs, etc.*
- *operates computerised records*
- *manages the return of items to the right location*
- *advises readers, finds information and reserves books from other libraries*
- *develops the stock of books, tapes, etc.*

Additional responsibilities
- *monitors the behaviour of people in the library*
- *manages the catalogue and access to the Internet*
- *collects money for late books*

Line Manager:

Job description 2

Job Title:

General responsibilities
Responsible for the operation of a check-out.

Main responsibilities
- *operates a till, swipes items to register price*
- *weighs and prices items sold by weight*
- *collects payment and gives change*
- *monitors the cash in the till*

Additional responsibilities
- *greets customers*
- *answers queries and advises customers*
- *packs customers' shopping*

Line Manager:

14.3

Mr Don't Know

LEVEL
Upper-intermediate

TOPIC
Recruiting people

ACTIVITY TYPE
Paired text analysis

WRITING FOCUS
Employment reference; emphasising ambiguity

TIME
50 minutes

KEY LANGUAGE
ambiguous, colleagues, confidential reference, conscientious, enthusiasm, to get rid of, punctuality, referee, reliability, to retain

PREPARATION
One photocopy, cut up, for each pair of students

Optionally, one photocopy of Writing style 1 (p.125) for each student

Warm up

1 Explain to the students that they want to apply for a job. They need two people who will recommend them, referees. Ask: *Who would you ask to be your referee?* Elicit how one referee is normally your current employer and the other someone who can give a character reference.

2 Brainstorm what is included in a confidential employer's reference, i.e. details of what a person does for their current company and how well they do it.

3 Elicit why an employer might not give a terrible employee a terrible confidential reference, i.e. to get rid of them. Elicit why an employer might not give an excellent employee an excellent reference, i.e. to retain them.

Main activity

1 Write this sentence on the board: *His attitude to work was consistent.* Explain that this sentence was written in a reference. Ask: *Is it positive or negative?* Elicit how it is actually ambiguous – his attitude could have been consistently bad! Elicit what inference the writer wants the reader to draw from this ambiguity, i.e. that they cannot whole-heartedly recommend the person. Brainstorm what a positive reference might say, e.g. *He works consistently hard.*

2 In pairs, give each pair a copy of the Mr Right or Mr Don't Know? statements. Tell the students to discuss the statements, decide if they are positive or ambiguous and fill in the boxes. Feedback as a whole class.

> **Suggested answer**
> **Positive:** 3, 6 (however the praise has been weakened by *quite* and *overall*), 4
> **Ambiguous:** 1, 2 (the *impact/contribution* could be uniquely or significantly bad!), 5, 7, 8 (each positive initial phrase is undermined by what follows)

3 Write a job on the board and brainstorm its related duties and responsibilities. Explain that the students are going to write a reference for an employee who has been doing the job. In groups of four, tell the students to choose a name for the employee.

4 Write on the board these categories: *punctuality, honesty, enthusiasm, reliability, attitude to customers, attitude to colleagues.* Tell the groups to quickly decide whether the employee rates as bad, OK or good in each of these categories. Explain that, using this information, they must decide if they want to retain this employee or get rid of them.

5 Give each group two copies of the Reference Template. Highlight how the information is typically structured, i.e. who the person is, what they do, what they are like, why they are leaving, whether you think they would be good at the new job and why. Also highlight the formal style and check any difficult vocabulary.

6 Split the groups into pairs. Ask the pairs to write their employee's reference, using the template to help them. You may want to give students a copy of Writing style 1 to help with this (see p.125).

7 After ten minutes, tell the groups to swap references and decide if they would employ the person described in the new references.

Follow up

- Ask the students to write a short questionnaire that a potential employer could send to check the facts about a person instead of asking for a reference.
- Ask the students to write the letter calling the candidate for interview.

Mr Right or Mr Don't Know?

1 His contribution to the company was unique.
2 He had a significant impact on the company.
3 I was quite impressed by her attitude to work.
4 She worked hard to overcome her lack of confidence when dealing with complaints.
5 He works with extreme care, taking as long as he needs to pay attention to the finest details.
6 Overall, he is a very conscientious employee.
7 Although her work was of a high standard, she found meeting deadlines a challenge.
8 She has the potential to be an excellent employee, but her attitude towards her colleagues could easily be misinterpreted.

Put the number for each statement in one of these boxes:

Positive	Ambiguous

 -

Reference Template

1 **Factual paragraph**

    e.g. *(Name)* has been employed by this company as *(Job title)*
        since *(date)*
        His/Her responsibilities included *(responsibilities)*
        Sentence indicating his/her success at the job

2 **Paragraph describing qualities and weaknesses**

3 **Paragraph saying**

    • *why the person is leaving*

        e.g. *(Name)* has sadly decided to move on as, at present, there
            is no opportunity for promotion within our company.

    • *giving a brief summary of paragraph 2*

    • *recommending / not recommending him/her for the job*

        e.g. I would (not) hesitate to recommend *(name)* for the post
            of *(new job's title)*.

Credit cards

LEVEL

Elementary

TOPIC

Borrowing money

ACTIVITY TYPE

Paired simulation

WRITING FOCUS

Form, semi-formal letter (request)

TIME

50 minutes

KEY LANGUAGE

to borrow money,
to buy things,
a credit card,
a credit limit,
to repay money;

Ways of expressing the future – *will, going to,* etc.

PREPARATION

One photocopy, cut up, for each student

Warm up

1   Mime borrowing a pen from a student and then giving it back. Elicit that you are not taking it but borrowing it. Ask: *I want €10,000. Who can I borrow it from?* Elicit the vocabulary *bank* and *credit card*.

2   Give each student a copy of the Credit Card Application Form and ask them to complete it quickly. If students feel uneasy about using their own details, tell them to write fictional ones. If any students find the form-filling difficult, ask stronger students to help them.

Main activity

1   After five minutes, draw a smiley face on the board: ☺. Explain that the bank has given all the students credit cards. Change the mouth to a sad face ☹. Explain that they have a credit limit of only €1,000. Ask: *What can we do?*

2   Explain that you have decided to write to the bank and ask for a higher credit limit. Tell them to decide how much they want: €10,000, €100,000 or €1,000,000.

3   Give each student a copy of the Letter. Elicit where they should put their address, the date and their name. Explain that this is the normal layout for a letter and that *Dear Sir or Madam / Yours faithfully* is used because they do not know the name of the person they are writing to. Tell them to cross out the two amounts of money that they do not want to borrow, and to edit the other parts of the letter so it makes sense. Feedback as a whole class.

4   In pairs, ask the students to brainstorm three very expensive things they would like to buy. Tell them to decide how much money they need to buy them and write their own letter to the credit card company asking for an increased credit limit.

5   After ten minutes, tell the pairs to swap their letters. Explain that they work for the bank. Tell them to read the new letter and underline anything that they do not believe or understand. Ask them to decide if it is a good application.

6   Tell the pairs to join into groups of four. Ask them to feedback to each other, explaining why they will or will not increase the other pair's credit limit.

Follow up

● Tell the students to write to a relative asking for help to repay their credit card.

● Explain to the students that they have a friend who keeps borrowing money but cannot repay it. Tell them to write a letter giving them some advice.

Credit Card Application Form

Section 1

Personal details

Mr ☐   Mrs ☐   Miss ☐   Ms ☐

First name ☐

Surname ☐

Date of birth: day ☐ month ☐ year ☐

Address ☐

Postcode ☐

Employment details

I am: employed ☐   a student ☐

Name of company/school/college ☐

Signature ☐   Today's date ☐

✂ -

Letter

[*Your address*]

[*Receiver's name and address*]   [*Today's date*]

Dear Sir or Madam

Account number 4568 3516 1230 1212

I would like to increase my credit limit to €10,000/€100,000/€1,000,000. I need this money to buy a new house / limousine / painting by Van Gogh / ring for my partner.

This is important to me because my house is very old / I want people to think I am famous / I want people to think I am rich / I want to marry them.

I will repay it by getting another job / borrowing money from another credit card / robbing a bank / selling my brother.

Thank you for your help.

Yours faithfully

[*Your signature and name*]

15.2

LEVEL
Intermediate

TOPIC
Returning faulty goods

ACTIVITY TYPE
Paired text analysis

WRITING FOCUS
Form, semi-formal letter (complaint); error correction

TIME
50 minutes

KEY LANGUAGE
Language of complaining; *mail order, order form, receipt, refund, 30-day money back guarantee, vase*

PREPARATION
One photocopy, cut up, for each student; one photocopy of the Second draft correction code (p.120) for each student

Optionally for Warm up, two pages from a variety of mail order gift catalogues for each pair of students. These do not have to be in English.

Optionally, one photocopy of Writing style 1 (p.125) for each student

Shopping by post

Warm up

1 Give each student a copy of the Order Form. Elicit what kind of form it is and whether any students have shopped by post. Ask: *Were you happy with the thing you bought? Were there any problems?* Elicit what a *30-day money back guarantee* is and how the company has included an example entry on the form to help the customer, i.e. the clock.

2 Put the students in pairs. Ask them to think of the perfect present for their partner and complete the Order Form. Explain that it will be posted direct to their partner and they must give them the completed Order Form so they can check it when it arrives! Alternatively, if you have brought in catalogues, give each pair two pages from the catalogues. Explain they must choose a good present for their partner and complete the Order Form. Tell them to tear out the present from the catalogue and give it to their partner.

Main activity

1 Explain that someone called Marta has also been given a present from the catalogue. In pairs, give out one copy of Letter 1 per student. Ask them to answer these questions: *1 Why is Marta writing to Cambridge Mail Order Ltd? 2 What was she given? 3 What is wrong with it? 4 What does she want the company to do?*

> **Answer key**
> 1 Because her friend bought her a present from the company.
> 2 A Greek flower vase
> 3 It is damaged.
> 4 She wants them to replace it.

2 Ask: *Is the letter easy to understand?* Elicit how it communicates but lacks organisation. Ask the students to reorganise the letter to make it clearer, following the order of the answers in step 1. Ask them to cross out anything that they think is not important. Feedback as a whole class.

3 Write on the board this summary:

> Dear Sir or Madam
>
> My friend buyed a berthday present from Cambridge Mail Order Ltd. Is a Greek vase.
>
> Is broke. I no have the recipe. I no want money but want a new vase.
>
> Love
> Marta

4 Give each student a copy of the Second draft correction code and ask them to work together to correct the summary. Feedback as a whole class. Elicit how this is a personal business letter and should be semi-formal in style. Brainstorm ways of rephrasing the letter to make it slightly more formal, e.g. using *would like* instead of *want,* and changing *Love* to *Yours faithfully.*

5 Give each student a copy of Letter 2. Read it together and elicit how the information is structured, i.e. what Marta got, what is wrong, what she wants done. Ask them to use the same structure to write a letter to the company about the present they were given in the Warm up, which has also broken. You may want to give students a copy of Writing style 1 to help them with this (see p.125).

6 After five minutes, ask them to swap letters with another student. Ask them to read their partner's letter and use the Second draft correction code to annotate any errors and then feedback to their partner. They should then correct their own letter.

Follow up

- Ask the students to write the letter from Cambridge Mail Order Ltd explaining what they are going to do about the broken present.

Cambridge Mail Order Ltd
Order Form
Order Address: Cambridge Mail Order Ltd
          PO Box 1124, Cambridge CB2 2RU

Mr/Mrs/Miss/Ms

Address

Postcode

Daytime phone

Catalogue Number	Quantity	Description of Item	Price £ p	Total £ p
T567/56	1	*Example: Green kitchen clock*	7 50	7 50

Please debit my Visa/Mastercard no.

Card expiry date

Cheques payable to **Cambridge Mail Order Ltd**
30-day money back guarantee

Total cost

Please add £2.95 delivery charge | 2 | 95 |
Total payment

Cardholder's signature

Letter 1

73 Queens Road
London W7 3EE

Cambridge Mail Order Ltd
PO Box 1124
Cambridge CB2 2RU

24 September 2004

Dear Sir or Madam

Is a Greek vase. Is broke. I no want money but want a new vase. Is relly special to me. Although he is cheap, I like because is of my friend. I no know exactly how it costed because I no have the recipe. My friend buyed from Cambridge Mail Order Ltd. Is a berthday present.

Love

Marta

Letter 2

73 Queens Road
London W7 3EE

Cambridge Mail Order Ltd
PO Box 1124
Cambridge CB2 2RU

24 September 2004

Dear Sir or Madam

My friend recently gave me a Greek flower vase which he bought from Cambridge Mail Order Ltd. When I opened it, I found it was broken. Unfortunately, I do not have a receipt.

As it was a special present I do not want a refund but I would like a replacement vase.

Many thanks for your help.

Yours faithfully

Marta Fernandez

15.3

LEVEL
Upper-intermediate

TOPIC
Delaying payment

ACTIVITY TYPE
Paired simulation

WRITING FOCUS
Formal letter
(responding to
demands, making
excuses)

TIME
50 minutes

KEY LANGUAGE
amount due, bill,
to break down,
cash-flow problems,
cheque, to cover,
invoice, payment,
receipt, reference,
signatures

PREPARATION
One photocopy, cut up,
for each pair of
students

Optionally, one
photocopy of Writing
style 1 (p.125) for each
student

Can't pay; won't pay!

Warm up

1   Brainstorm methods of payment that students routinely use, e.g. cash, cheque, credit card, etc. Ask: *Do businesses buy things this way?* Elicit how businesses usually agree terms to pay later.

2   In pairs, give each pair a copy of the Letter. Ask them to find one word in the letter which means a document that asks for payment at an agreed time in the future. (Answer: *invoice*) Elicit the difference in meaning between this, a *bill*, which requests immediate payment, and a *receipt*, which shows you have paid for something.

Main activity

1   Ask what the letter is about. (Answer: SL Insurance Ltd has bought some office furniture but failed to pay the invoice at the agreed time.) In pairs, ask the students to complete the exercise. Feedback as a whole class.

> **Answer key**
> a 9   b 1   c 8   d 3   e 4   f 2   g 7   h 6   i 5

Elicit how Stafford Office Furniture do not want to lose future custom from SL Insurance and how the general level of formality, tentative use of *seem to* and closing polite request are used to try to soften the request for payment.

2   Tell the students that they work in the Accounts Department of SL Insurance Ltd. Write on the board: *They're very polite! They can wait. Make some excuse. MF* Explain that this note from the Managing Director was attached to the letter. Elicit its meaning and why Mr Finch might want to pay late, e.g. *he has cash-flow problems.*

3   Give each pair a set of Excuses cards. Ask them to read the excuses and write two more possible excuses on the blank cards.

4   Ask the pairs to swap their Excuses cards with another pair and spread the new set face down over their desk. Tell them to turn one over at random. Explain they must write a polite letter to Stafford Office Furniture Ltd, using this excuse, to explain why they have not been paid.

5   Brainstorm useful formal phrases and write them on the board, e.g. *Please accept our apologies; We very much regret …; This late payment is due to the fact …,* etc.

6   In pairs, ask the students to write the letter. You may want to give students a copy of Writing style 1 to help them with this (see p.125).

7   When they have had sufficient time, ask them to swap their letter with another pair, read the new letter and decide if they accept the excuse. If it is unacceptable, they should decide what action to take.

8   Ask the pairs to join together in groups of four and explain how much longer they will give the company to pay or what action they have decided to take next.

Follow up

●   Ask the students to write a second, stronger letter from Stafford Office Furniture Ltd demanding payment.

●   Tell the students to write a letter from Stafford Office Furniture Ltd to a potential new customer explaining their terms, i.e. how and when they should be paid.

Letter

¹ *Stafford Office Furniture Ltd*

Alsager Road, Stafford, ST1 2LL

Tel: 01763 244800   **Fax:** 01763 244888   **Email:** enquiries@staffurn.co.uk

```
³ Mr M Finch                                    ² 14 July 2004
  Managing Director
  SL Insurance Ltd
  PO Box 482
  Cambridge CB1 1AN




⁴ Our Ref. LP1/LL
⁵ Dear Mr Finch
⁶ Re: Invoice no. 125682   Amount due £1,650.05
⁷ We do not seem to have received payment to cover this invoice. We would
  be grateful if you could send payment as soon as possible. If you have
  already paid, or have a reason not to pay, please phone us.

⁸ Yours sincerely


⁹ Ms L. Lewis

  Ms L. Lewis
```

Where are these things? Match each lettered item to a number in the letter:

a a signature ....

b the sender's address ....

c words to close the letter ....

d the receiver's name and address ....

e a reference ....

f the date ....

g most important information ....

h what the letter is about ....

i words to open the letter ....

✂ Excuses

We have not received the invoice.	Mr Finch is away and no-one else can sign the cheque.
We sent the cheque last week.	Our computer has broken down.

16.1

One thing led to another ...

LEVEL
Elementary

TOPIC
Planning stories

ACTIVITY TYPE
Group game

WRITING FOCUS
Fiction; plotting a story

TIME
50 minutes

KEY LANGUAGE
crown, dominoes, fairy godmother, magic wand, pattern, prince, problem, slipper;
Past tenses

PREPARATION
One photocopy, cut up, of set of Cinderella Cards and Instant Plot Card for each pair of students; one set of Plotting Dominoes, cut up, for each group of four students

Optionally, a simplified photocopy of the First draft checklist (p.120) for each student

Note: If your students are not likely to know the Cinderella story, go straight to the Main activity

You can download other world folk stories at www.pitt.edu/~dash/folktexts.html

Warm up

1 Draw a glass slipper, a magic wand and a crown on the board. Ask: *What is the story?* Elicit the name Cinderella. Ask: *At the start of the story, what is Cinderella's problem?* (Answer: she is poor and cannot go to a party.)

2 In pairs, give each pair a set of Cinderella cards and ask them to put them in the right order. Feedback as a whole class.

> **Answer key**
> d, a, c, b

3 Give each pair an Instant Plot Card and ask them to put it above the Cinderella Cards. Elicit how the story of Cinderella has this pattern: a problem (d), an answer (a) which makes another problem (c), and then a final solution (b).

Main activity

1 In groups of four, give each group one set of Plotting Dominoes. Explain they are going to tell their own group story, and encourage them to use their imaginations.

2 Ask each student to take three dominoes at random. Ask Student 1 to choose one of their dominoes and place it on the desk. Ask them to explain what is happening in the picture and what the character's problem is, making the story as interesting as possible. Tell the group to give the people on the card names and discuss what they think their lives are like.

3 Ask Student 2 to choose one of their dominoes and put it next to Student 1's, explaining what the answer to the problem is and how the character responds. Emphasise that they only have one minute to talk about each card, they must use their imaginations and any answer, as long as it is believable, is correct. Student 3 must then continue the story with another domino problem, which Student 4 must give another domino answer to. Student 1 then continues the same story with another problem, and the students continue the line until they have used all their dominoes. After twelve minutes ask the students to finish their domino story with a final solution.

4 Ask the groups to choose the best four-domino section of their group's line and place those dominoes under an Instant plot card to help them remember the problem-answer-problem-answer pattern.

5 Split the groups into two pairs. Tell the pairs they have ten minutes to use this four-domino section as the basis of a 60–80-word story, which they should make as interesting as possible.

6 When the students have had enough time, ask them to swap stories with the other pair in their group. Ask them to read the story to see how it differs from their own story.

7 Ask the pairs to join back together as groups of four, decide which of the two stories is the most interesting and how the students could improve both stories. You may want to give students a simplified copy of the First draft checklist to help them with this (see p.120).

8 Ask the pairs to redraft their stories.

Follow up

● Ask the students to write a story of only 50 words, based on something that really happened to them. Tell them to use the problem-answer-problem-answer pattern.

● Ask the students to choose a story genre, e.g. love, horror, science fiction, etc. and write a problem-answer-problem-answer story using someone famous as the main character.

Cinderella Cards

d

Cinderella was too poor to go to the party.

a

The Fairy Godmother helped Cinderella go to the party. Cinderella fell in love with the Prince.

c

At midnight, Cinderella left quickly. She thought she would never see the Prince again.

b

The Prince found Cinderella. They got married and she became rich.

Instant Plot Card

Problem ➡ Answer **but** Problem ➡ Answer

Plotting Dominoes

16.2

The six friends

LEVEL
Intermediate

TOPIC
Inventing fictional answers

ACTIVITY TYPE
Group role play

WRITING FOCUS
Personal letter (explanatory); varying viewpoint

KEY LANGUAGE
crime, criminal, disappearance, to get hold of (someone), in touch, mobile (phone), nightmare, victim;
Past and future tenses

TIME
50 minutes

PREPARATION
For the Warm up: a photograph / magazine picture of an unknown person, ripped into four pieces.
One photocopy, cut up, for each pair of students

Note: If you have access to computers, you can get the students to link their letters into a narrative using hyperlinks

Warm up

1 Stick the torn photograph or magazine picture you brought with you on to the board without explanation. Write: *1 What? 2 How? 3 Why? 4 Who? 5 When?* Allow students to create their own answers.

> **Suggested answer**
> (**1**) A photo (**2**) ripped (**3**) in anger when (**4**) your boyfriend/girlfriend (**5**) left you.

2 Show how they have created a history for the object from nothing. Explain that these questions are five of a writer's best friends and we normally answer at least three of them in any piece of writing. Elicit what the writer's sixth friend is. (Answer: Where?)

Main activity

1 In pairs, give each pair a copy of the Letter and brainstorm the relationship between Sue, the writer, and Carol, the recipient. (Answer: a close friend or relative) Tell the students to identify the four questions which are answered in the letter and make notes in the question boxes. Feedback as a whole class.

> **Answer key**
> **What?** The police have questioned Sue.
> **Where?** The police station
> **When?** In the night
> **Who?** The police want to find out about Adam.

2 Ask: *Why do the police want to find out about Adam?* Elicit answers from the students, making sure you include the possibility that Adam is a criminal and/or is in some kind of danger.

3 Split the class into two groups, A and B. Give each student in group A a copy of Role Card A, and each student in group B a copy of Role Card B. In their groups, tell them to discuss the questions in Part 1 of their Role Card.

4 After five minutes, split the groups into pairs and ask them to write the letter described in Part 2 of their role card. Tell them to ensure to include some information from Part 1 and answer all three questions from Part 2.

5 When the students have had enough time, ask them to swap their letter with a pair from the other group. Ask them to read the new letter and decide what has happened to Adam, according to the letter. Explain that both groups had the same questions for Part 2. Tell them to check that all three questions have been sufficiently well answered in the new letter and underline anything they feel is unclear or needs to be expanded.

6 Ask the pairs to join with the pair who has their letter and discuss what they think has happened to Adam, according to the letter they have just read, and any corrections they feel need to be made.

7 Ask the pairs to take back their original letter and correct it.

Follow up

- Ask the students to write the three questions Adam would answer in his letter to Sue explaining what has happened. They should then write his letter.

- Ask the students to write a letter to a pen pal or friend describing the most exciting, frightening or interesting thing that has happened to them recently.

Letter

Dear Carol

I've been trying to phone you but you're never home and your mobile's constantly switched off! You won't believe it – the most terrible thing has happened. The police came in the middle of the night. It was like a nightmare with them banging on my door.

They took me to the Police Station and kept asking about Adam, but I haven't seen him since last night. He left without even saying goodbye. You know what he's like, never in one place for more than five minutes. They just wouldn't believe me.

They let me go after a couple of hours and made me promise I'd ring them if he got in touch. Please come as soon as you can.

Love
Sue

Questions
What?
Where?
When?
Who?

Role Cards

A

Adam is a criminal

Part 1. Decide on answers to these questions:

What was Adam's crime? When did he do it? Why has he disappeared?

Part 2. You are the victim of Adam's crime. Write a letter to a close friend. In the letter you must explain some of the facts in Part 1 and answer these questions:

How do you feel about Adam's disappearance? Why do you feel that way? What are you going to do next?

B

Adam is in some kind of danger

Part 1. Decide on answers to these questions:

Who wants to get hold of Adam? Why do they want to get hold of Adam? What will they do?

Part 2. You are one of the people who are trying to get hold of Adam. Write a letter to a close friend. In the letter you must explain some of the facts in Part 1 and answer these questions:

How do you feel about Adam's disappearance? Why you do feel that way? What are you going to do next?

16.3

The storyteller

LEVEL:
Upper-intermediate

TOPIC:
Memorable events retold

ACTIVITY TYPE:
Group storytelling

WRITING FOCUS:
Fiction; drafting

TIME:
50 minutes

KEY LANGUAGE:
to focus on something, to highlight something, location, memorable, recognisable;
Past tenses

PREPARATION:
One photocopy, cut up, for each student

Note: The activity described is for groups of four students; for uneven numbered groups see Note after step 8

Warm up

Explain to the students that they are going to tell their own stories in this lesson. Give each student a copy of the Story Cues and tell them they have five minutes to complete the cue sentences. Ideally they should write about themselves but if they get stuck on any of them they can be creative with their memories!

Main activity

1 Put the students in groups of four. Give each student a number, 1–4. Ask Student 1 to work with Student 2 and Student 3 to work with Student 4. (See note after step 8 for working with uneven numbered groups of students.)

2 In their pairs, ask the students to swap their Story Cues and read them. Tell Student 2 to choose Student 1's most interesting sentence and ask them to tell the story behind it. At the same time ask Student 4 to choose one story which Student 3 must tell. Explain they only have five minutes. While Student 2 and Student 4 are listening they should not make notes.

> **Telling the story**
> S1 ——▶ S2
> S3 ——▶ S4

3 After five minutes, stop the students and repeat step 2, this time with Student 1 and 3 doing the choosing and Student 2 and Student 4 doing the telling.

4 After five minutes, stop the students. Explain that they now 'own' the story they have just heard. They can change anything and expand it to make it their own work of fiction.

> **Telling the story**
> S2 ——▶ S1
> S4 ——▶ S3

5 Give each student a copy of The First Draft. Explain they have ten minutes to write their new version of the other student's story, using the notes to help them. Ask them to write in the first person and give the story a definite beginning, middle and end, and ensure it involves at least three characters.

6 After ten minutes stop the students. Ask Student 1 to swap their written story with Student 3. Ask Student 2 to swap their written story with Student 4. Give them five minutes to read the new story.

7 Give each student a copy of The Second Draft. Tell them they have ten minutes to write their version of the new story and redraft it, using the notes to help them.

8 After ten minutes, tell them to pass both the first and second drafts back to the person who originally told the story. Tell them to read the drafts and discuss in the group how the stories have changed and whether they have improved or not.

> **Note**: If you have to make a group of three, ask two students initially to work as a pair. In this case Student 1 tells Student 2 and Student 3 one story. Student 2 and Student 3 tell Student 1 one story each and Student 1 must select which they want to write. The students now work individually writing the first drafts. In step 6, the first draft is passed to the other students like this: S1 ——▶ S2 ——▶ S3 ——▶ S1.
> If you have only five students, put them into one group of three and one of two. The group of two should follow the procedure for Student 1 and Student 2 in steps 2 and 3 above.

Follow up

- Ask the students to choose one of the other three Story Cues they listed in the Warm up. Ask them to write a 200–300 word story based on it, using both sets of the Ideas for developing first and second drafts.

- Ask the students to choose a recent news story and retell it as if they had been present at the event. Ask them to use the drafting ideas to help them add interest.

Story Cues

1   The scariest thing that has happened to me is ....

....

2   The first time I ....

....

3   My worst day was when ....

....

4   I thought I could never ....

.... but I did!

✂ -

The First Draft

Beginning: *Put the story in a location you know. Add details that make the reader feel they also know the location, even if they have never been there.*

Middle: *Highlight a problem. Make it the focus of the story. Make the reader know how important it is to the people in the story.*

End: *Solve the problem.*

✂ -

The Second Draft

Beginning: *Make the opening sentence catch the reader's interest.*

Middle: *Make the reader care about the people. Briefly describe them and add details to make them similar to people you know.*

End: *Make the last sentence strong and memorable.*

Short circuits

LEVEL
Elementary

TOPIC
Simple electrical
circuits

ACTIVITY TYPE
Paired game

**WRITING
FOCUS**
Sequenced
description

TIME
50 minutes

KEY LANGUAGE
*battery, bulb,
bulb holder, buzzer,
circuit, current,
doorbell, electric fan,
electric motor, to flow,
switch, wire;*

Sequencers;
prepositions of
movement: *from,
through, to, into*

PREPARATION
One photocopy, cut up,
for each pair of
students

Warm up

1   Draw this picture of a bulb with only one wire going to a battery.
    Do not draw the dotted line. Brainstorm the vocabulary and ask:
    What is this? Will it work?

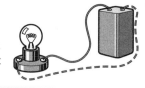

> **Answer key**
> It is an incomplete electrical circuit which includes a light.
> It will not work because it needs another wire to complete the circuit.

Draw in the missing wire – the dotted line – and elicit how electricity flows in a circle from
the battery, through the bulb and back to the battery.

2   Draw this electrical circuit diagram under the drawing and
    label it. Elicit which symbol represents which part of the circuit.
    (Answer: crossed circle = bulb, two vertical lines = battery,
    horizontal lines = wire)
    Explain that it is an easy way of drawing the circuit.

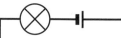

bulb + wire + battery + wire

Main activity

1   Put the students in pairs and give each pair a copy of the Circuit Description and a set of
    Circuit 1 cards, cut up. Tell them to read the description and put the cards in a circle to
    form a circuit. Explain that circuits always start at a battery or power source. Feedback as
    a whole class and explain that they have made a torch.

> **Suggested answer**
> 2, 4, 3, 4, 1, 4 ➔ 2, etc.

2   Give each pair a set of Circuit 2 and 3 cards, mixed up. Tell them to arrange the cards to
    make two circuits: an electric fan and a doorbell. Feedback as a whole class.

> **Answer key**
> **Electric fan**: c, a, b, a, d, a ➔ c, etc.
> **Doorbell**: c, a, b, a, e, a ➔ c, etc.

Elicit how the switch for a doorbell is normally a button which you push, not switch, to
complete the circuit.

3   Tell the students to reread the Circuit Description, underline all the verbs and say which
    tense they are in. Feedback as a whole class. Explain that the present simple tense is used
    as the process does not change and is always true.

4   Tell the students to find sequencers in the description that mean *next, at the same time,*
    and *last*. Feedback as a whole class. (Answer: *then, as, finally*)

5   In pairs, tell the students to write a similar description of how either a fan or a doorbell
    works. Explain they should use the circuits they made in step 2 to help them.

6   Tell the pairs to swap their description with another pair. Tell them to read the new
    description and underline anything that they think is unclear or confusing and add
    sequencers, if necessary.

7   Tell the students to swap back their descriptions and discuss and correct the things that
    have been underlined.

Follow up

• Brainstorm the water cycle and draw a diagram on the board (i.e. rain falling from
  clouds onto the land, draining into a river, then into the sea, the sun heating the sea,
  water vapour rising, making clouds, rain falling, etc.). Ask the students to write a
  description of the water cycle, beginning with *Rain falls … .*

• Write on the board: *How circuits work.* Tell the students to create a poster to help
  young children understand how circuits work. They can use their description, a circuit
  diagram and any other illustrations they think will help.

Circuit Description

How a torch works

When the switch is on, an electric current flows from a battery through a wire to the switch. It then flows through another wire to a bulb. As it passes through the bulb it lights it. The current finally flows through a third wire, back to the battery.

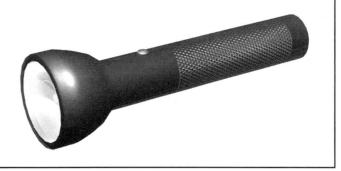

Circuit 1

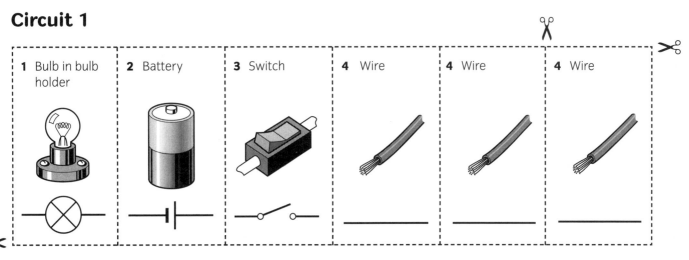

| 1 Bulb in bulb holder | 2 Battery | 3 Switch | 4 Wire | 4 Wire | 4 Wire |

Circuits 2 and 3

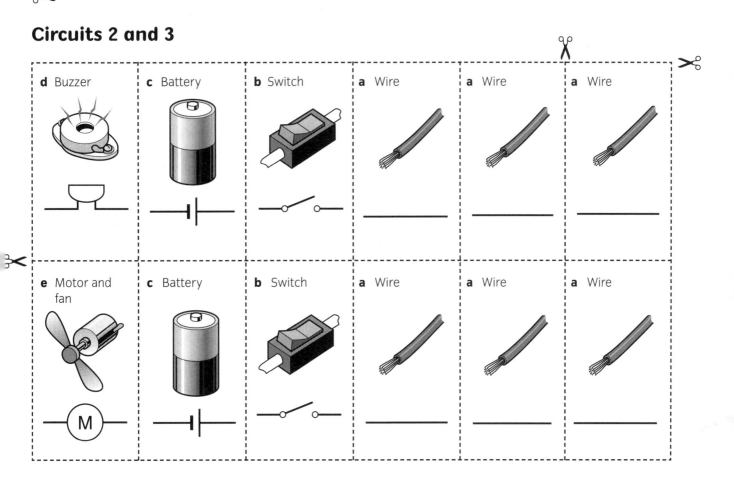

| d Buzzer | c Battery | b Switch | a Wire | a Wire | a Wire |
| e Motor and fan | c Battery | b Switch | a Wire | a Wire | a Wire |

17.2

It's amazing ...

LEVEL
Intermediate

TOPIC
Selling new
inventions

ACTIVITY TYPE
Pair simulation

**WRITING
FOCUS**
Catalogue
descriptions

TIME
50 minutes

KEY LANGUAGE
*computer mouse,
fast food, to fill a bath,
to invent, invention,
inventor, keyboard,
to plug into,
to be powered by,
a selling point*

PREPARATION
One photocopy, cut
up, for each pair of
students; one
photocopy of the First
draft checklist (p.120)
for each pair of
students

Warm up

1   Write the name *Alexander Graham Bell* on the board and draw a telephone. Elicit how
they are connected and the vocabulary *inventor, invention* and *to invent something.*

2   Put the class into pairs and give each pair one copy of Inventor's Notes a (In-car oven) and the
four Catalogue Pictures. Tell them to match the notes to one of the pictured inventions.

> **Answer key**
> Picture 1

Main activity

1   Write these questions on the board: *How useful is it? How interesting is it? How easy will
it be to sell?* Tell the pairs to reread the notes and rank the in-car oven from 1 to 10 (1 = not
at all, 10 = very) for each of these questions. Feedback as a whole class by totalling the
numbers from each pair and dividing them to get an average for each question.
Brainstorm why people might buy the oven, i.e. its main selling points.

2   Explain that your company is going to put the oven in its mail order catalogue. Tell the
students you can only use 30 words to 'sell it' to the reader. Brainstorm the characteristics
of such catalogue descriptions, i.e. products are described in an informative but friendly
style, using concise sentences which state why the reader needs that particular product.
As a whole class, create the catalogue description on the board.

> **Suggested answer**
> No time to stop to eat? Use this amazing in-car oven while you're on the move.
> Simply plug it into your cigarette lighter and you'll have warm snacks in seconds!

3   In their pairs give each pair a copy of one of the remaining Inventor's Notes, i.e. pair 1,
note b; pair 2, note c, etc. Ask them to match the invention in their notes to one of the
three remaining Catalogue Pictures.

4   Ask the students to identify their invention's main selling points and, in their pairs, write
the 30-word catalogue description for it. Once the students have completed their first
draft, if there is time, ask them to swap it with another pair which has the same invention.
Ask them to check the other pair's description, using the First draft checklist, and mark
where improvements could be made. After a few minutes, ask them to swap back and if
necessary, redraft their own description, using the other pair's comments to help them.

5   If possible, combine the pairs into groups of six, each of which contains one pair 1, 2 and 3.
Ask the pairs within the groups to swap their catalogue descriptions. If the class does not
easily divide this way, work as a whole class and display the catalogue descriptions on the
board or walls. Ask the pairs to find and read the descriptions of the two other products
illustrated in the pictures, ranking them from 1 to 10 as they did for the in-car oven.
Feedback as a whole class and select one invention to feature on the catalogue's cover.

Follow up

● Ask the students to think of an invention that would really help them in their daily life,
e.g. a homework machine and write a catalogue description of it.

● Explain that the company wants to get some publicity for its new catalogue. Ask the
students to write a press release for the invention the class chose for the catalogue's
cover. This press release will be sent out to newspapers and should include: a headline
that will catch the editor's interest; a brief description of the product that emphasises its
uniqueness and the benefits to the consumer; how people can buy the product; and a
contact phone number or e-mail address.

Catalogue Pictures

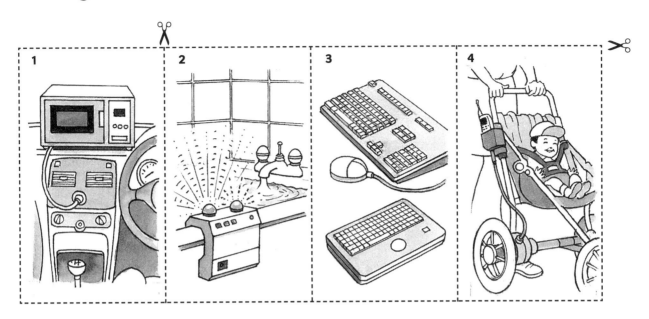

Inventor's Notes

a
In-car oven
Whole class

People are busy and need 'fast food'. Getting food from cafés takes a long time. People eat meals in their cars. They need an oven they can use in their car. It needs to be plugged into the cigarette lighter. It could be used for picnics.

b
Bath flood alarm
Pair 1

People leave baths filling with water while they do something else. They waste money by filling them with too much water. Overflowing baths can cause floods and damage the house. People need an alarm on the side of the bath that goes off when water touches it.

c
Kid's keyboard
Pair 2

Young children use computers. Young children have small fingers. Small fingers need small keys. Parents want to help their children. Parents have big fingers. You need two keyboards. A 'mouse' is difficult to use for children. It needs to be smaller and part of the keyboard.

d
Buggy phone charger
Pair 3

Parents of babies need a phone in an emergency. Mobile phones need batteries. Batteries run out. If their mobiles don't work, they could have problems. Lots of parents push baby buggies. Wheels can make electricity as they turn. Baby buggies' wheels could recharge mobile phones or other batteries.

17.3

www.worldwideweb?

LEVEL
Upper-intermediate

TOPIC
Access to the
Internet

ACTIVITY TYPE
Interpreting data

**WRITING
FOCUS**
Comparative report;
describing changes
and trends

TIME
50 minutes

KEY LANGUAGE
*to bottom out, to
decrease, to fall back,
to level off, to peak,
to remain steady, to
rise by/to, to rocket,
to slump, a trend,
to trough*

PREPARATION
One photocopy, cut up,
for each student

Warm up

1 Elicit what percentage of the class use the Internet.

2 Write on the board: *1% (1991)* and *45% (2000)*. Brainstorm what these numbers mean. (Answer: percentage of population who use the Internet in the USA)

3 Write on the board: *57 (1990)* and *110 (2000)*. Explain that these show the numbers of telephone lines per 100 people in the USA. Ask: *Is there any link between these two sets of numbers?* (Answer: Yes, because you need a telephone connection to use the Internet! When more people wanted to use the Internet, more telephone lines were created.)

Main activity

1 Give each student a copy of the Graph. Elicit if there are any trends.

2 Give each student a copy of the Comparative Report. Ask them to read it and check if they identified the trends correctly. While they are reading, draw this table on the board. Do not write the words in italics or the dashes.

↑	↓	→	⌣	⌢
to rocket	to slump	to level off	to bottom out	*to peak*
to rise	to come down	*to remain steady*	–	–
to increase	*to decrease*	–	–	–
to grow	*to fall (back)*	–	–	–

Ask the students to complete the table using verbs from the Comparative Report. Feedback as a whole class.

3 Highlight the last sentence in the report: *In 1998 the number of lines continued to decrease and by 2000 the number had fallen by 0.48 lines to 4.58 lines per 100 people.* Emphasise: *fall to* (a total) and *fall by* (a difference).

4 Draw this table on the board. Do not write those adverbs in italics. Ask the students to complete it using the adverbs from the report. Feedback.

Adverbs of change	
a little	**a lot**
slowly	sharply
slightly	*significantly*
gradually	*dramatically*

5 In pairs, ask the students to write the next two paragraphs of the report, one for Albania and one for Zimbabwe, and a general conclusion that covers all the countries.

6 After five minutes, ask the pairs to swap their report with another pair, check the new report for accuracy of information and feedback corrections to the other pair.

7 Ask the students to predict how many people have access to the Internet in the countries studied. Give each student a copy of the Table. Explain that no information is available for North Korea and Somalia. Tell them to check their predictions and write a comparative report based on the table that draws together information from the table and the graph. In their report ask them comment on what they believe the figures for North Korea and Somalia would indicate if they were available, and justify their comments.

Follow up

● Ask the students to find out about how the population of their country has changed over the last 100 years compared to the population of one other country and the world in general, and write a comparative report.

● Ask the students to write a discursive composition of 200 – 250 words based on this statement: *'The Internet will bring benefits to us all.'*

Graph

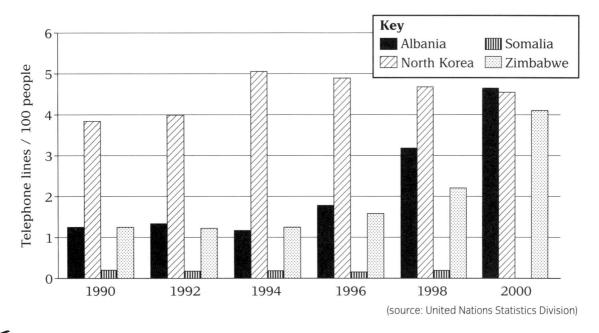

(source: United Nations Statistics Division)

Comparative Report

In general, in the period 1990 to 1996, the number of telephone lines per 100 people increased gradually for all countries. From 1998 to 2000 the number of lines grew dramatically in two of the four countries.

Although no figures for Somalia for 2000 are available, in that country the number of lines remained steady through the rest of the period, never rising significantly.

Figures for North Korea peaked at 5.06 lines per 100 people in 1994 before falling back in 1996 to 4.9. In 1998 the number of lines continued to decrease and by 2000 the number had fallen by 0.48 to 4.58 lines per 100 people.

(source: United Nations Statistics Division)

Table

Internet users per 100 population

Country	1994	1996	1998	2000
Albania	0	0.03	0.05	0.09
Zimbabwe	0	0.02	0.09	0.37
USA	4.99	16.95	31.3	45.07
World	0.36	1.27	3.07	6.33

(source: United Nations Statistics Division)

18.1

Planning problems

LEVEL
Elementary

TOPIC
A new bypass

ACTIVITY TYPE
Group simulation

WRITING FOCUS
Petition; expanding ideas

TIME
50 minutes

KEY LANGUAGE
argument, bypass,
to bypass, countryside,
lorries, migrating,
negative, petition,
plan, to plan
something, pollution,
positive, town, village

PREPARATION
Two photocopies, cut up, of the Map and the Petition Template for each group of four students; one set of Pros and Cons Cards, cut up, for each group of four students

Note: You can download other petitions from www.petitiononline.com

Warm up

Write on the board: *Why do we build new roads? How do you choose the best place for a new road?* Elicit answers, including the vocabulary *a bypass* and *to bypass a town.*

Main activity

1 Put the students in groups of four. Give each group two copies of the Map. Explain that they are going to look at plans for a new bypass in the south of England. Ask them to look at the map and elicit the name of a village, the name of a town and the route of the new road.

2 Give each group a set of Pros and Cons Cards. Ask them to find the + and – cards and put them on the desk. Ask them to mix up the others and put them face down.

3 Tell them they live in Hastings and are going to talk about the planned bypass. Explain they must take it in turns to turn over a card and discuss whether they think it contains a positive reason for building the new road or a negative argument against it. Tell them to put the card on the – or + pile. Repeat until they have three cards on one pile. They do not have to use all the cards. When they have a pile of three, check with each group that they understand their cards.

4 Explain that if they have three – cards they do not want the road built, if they have three + cards they do want it built. Tell them they are going to send a petition to the government, explaining their arguments for or against the bypass.

5 Tell the groups to answer these questions: *What do you think about the bypass? Why do you think it? What do you want?* Give each group two copies of the Petition Template and ask them, in pairs, to use these questions to help them complete the template.

6 Explain that now they need to get support for their petition. Tell them to walk around the classroom and try to get people to sign it. If they run out of space for signatures, tell them to continue on the back of the template.

7 Feedback as a whole class whether the bypass should go ahead or not. (In reality, 80% of Hastings' residents wanted the bypass, but the plan was rejected by the government in July 2001.)

Follow up

- Ask the students to write a similar petition about an issue that is important to their town or region or the place where they are studying. If they want to, students can publish their petitions online at www.petitiononline.com and see how much support they receive.

- Ask the students to write a letter to the local newspaper, explaining what they think about the bypass.

Map

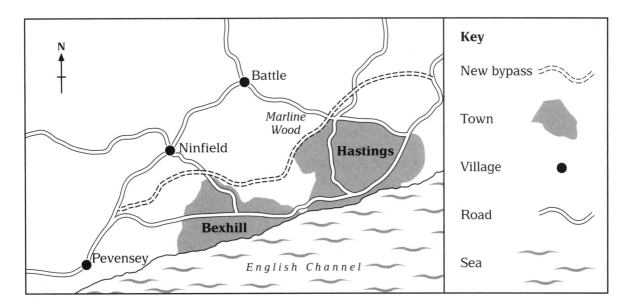

Pros and Cons Cards

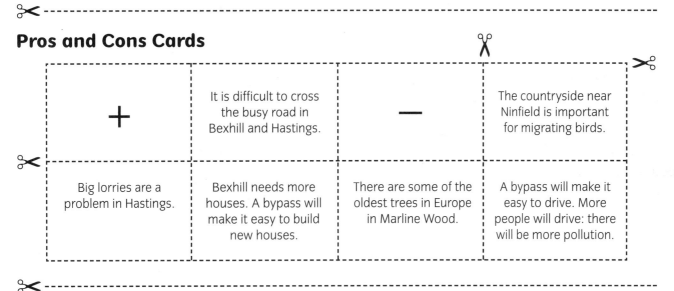

+	It is difficult to cross the busy road in Bexhill and Hastings.	—	The countryside near Ninfield is important for migrating birds.
Big lorries are a problem in Hastings.	Bexhill needs more houses. A bypass will make it easy to build new houses.	There are some of the oldest trees in Europe in Marline Wood.	A bypass will make it easy to drive. More people will drive: there will be more pollution.

Petition Template

To: The Prime Minister, 10 Downing Street, London, England SW1A 2AA

1. We think that …

2. We think this because …

3. We ask you to …

Signed:

Name	Signature

18.2

Campaign, not complain

LEVEL
Intermediate

TOPIC
Campaigning

ACTIVITY TYPE
Paired simulation

WRITING FOCUS
Semi-formal letter (protest)

TIME
50 minutes

KEY LANGUAGE
hostel, lack of support, playgroup, nuclear/renewable energy, pollution, radioactive leaks, risk;

Stating opinions:
I feel strongly that …, I can't believe that …, It is unbelievable that …

PREPARATION
One photocopy for each pair of students

Optionally, one photocopy of Writing style 1 (p.125) for each student

Note: add one local item as Dilemma number six before you photocopy them

Warm up

Write on the board: *… cheap power and only a small risk of radioactive leaks. The local people may cause problems if they find out so keep it quiet. I'll fax …* Explain that this was written on a scrap of paper that a friend who works for an electricity company passed to you. The friend cannot do anything because they think they will lose their job if they do. They think you can do something. Brainstorm what the document is about. (Answer: It is a part of a fax or letter about siting a nuclear power station nearby.)

Main activity

1   Write on the board: *nuclear/renewable energy*. Tell the students they have two minutes to write notes on the first thing that comes into their heads about these two types of energy. While they are doing this divide the board in two. Leave one half blank and on the other write the headings *Pros* and *Cons*. Feedback, writing the students' ideas under the two headings. Ensure you do not write on the other half of the board.

2   Ask: *What can we do about the scrap of document we've been given?*

3   Explain that you are going to write a letter to a newspaper about the proposed nuclear power station. Your letter will either be for or against it, depending on which of your lists is longest, pros or cons. As a whole class, elicit language used for giving opinions, e.g. *I feel strongly that …, I can't believe that …*, etc. and the structure of such a letter, i.e. a description of what is proposed, your opinion of it and what you feel should be done. Using the notes, write a 100-word letter on the board based on the structure of the Template. As you write, discuss the changes you make while drafting the letter, e.g. *Is this the most important point? Is this the best word? Is it formal enough?*, etc.

4   Put the students in groups of four. As a group, tell them to choose a number between one and six. Give each group two copies of the Dilemmas and Template. Ask them to read the dilemma that corresponds to the number they chose. As a group, ask them to brainstorm pros and cons for that dilemma and make prioritised notes.

5   Split the groups into two pairs. Ask Pair 1 to use one copy of the Template to write to the newspaper making positive points about the situation. Ask Pair 2 to use the other copy of the Template to write making negative points.

6   Tell Pair 1 to swap its letter with Pair 2 and vice versa. Ask them to read the new letter and check that it presents information clearly, logically and in an appropriate semi-formal style, underlining anything they feel needs to be changed. You may want to give students a copy of Writing style 1 to help with this (see p.125).

7   Join the pairs together and, if they need to, get them to redraft their letters. When they have had enough time, ask them to swap both their letters with another group.

8   Tell them to read the new letters from the other group and decide which one contains the most convincing arguments and why. One person from each group should then feedback their reasons to the other group.

Follow up

*   Ask the students to think of one subject that is important to them and write a letter about it to a local or national newspaper. They should select the newspaper carefully, writing only to one that would be interested in their subject.

*   Ask the students to write a discursive composition based on one of the class's letters, entitled: *'The problem with …'* .

Dilemmas

1 The factory which employs most of the people in your town is producing dangerous pollution.
2 A hostel for homeless drug addicts is going to be opened in your street.
3 A local playgroup for three-year-olds is closing because of lack of support from parents.
4 The noise from the nearby airport is increasing and makes it difficult to sleep.
5 The government wants to build 10,000 new houses near your quiet country village.
6 ....
   ....

Template

(Your address)

(Receiver's name and address)   *(The date)*

Dear Sir or Madam

I am writing about/concerning/regarding …   *(What is happening)*

Firstly,   *(Your most important point)*

In addition,   *(Your second most important point)*

In short,   *(Summary of what you want done)*

Yours faithfully

(Name)

18.3

Water: a clear solution

LEVEL
Upper-intermediate

TOPIC
Clean water,
development

ACTIVITY TYPE
Paired simulation

WRITING FOCUS
E-mail campaigning;
presenting opinion

TIME
50 minutes

KEY LANGUAGE
*catchment, communal,
consumption, donor,
down pipe, filter,
ground water,
guttering, to harvest,
outlet tap, storage tank*

PREPARATION
One photocopy, cut up,
for each student

Optionally, one photocopy
of Writing organisation 2
(p.124) for each student

Note: For more information
on DRWH visit
www.eng.warwick.ac.uk/dtu/
rwh/index.html

Warm up

1 Write these words in a column on the board: *fresh, dirty, tank, rain, pipe, consumption, filter, ground*. Elicit a word which collocates with all of them. (Answer: *water*) Brainstorm the word order of the collocations, i.e. *fresh water, dirty water, water tank, rain water, water pipe, water consumption, water filter, ground water*. Elicit what each means.

2 Write on the board: *One billion*. Brainstorm how students think this number is connected to water. (Answer: This is the number of people in the world who do not have access to clean water.)

Main activity

1 In pairs, give each pair a copy of the DRWH picture. Ask them to fill in the boxes with the correct words and discuss: *Why people harvest rain water; How clean/expensive they think it is; In which areas of the world it is a practical possibility*. Feedback as a whole class.

> **Answer key**
> **1** guttering   **2** down pipes   **3** storage tank   **4** outlet tap

2 Give each pair a copy of Water Facts. Explain that the facts are not in the most logical order; ask the students to read the list and arrange the facts more logically. Feedback as a whole class.

> **Suggested answer**
> 1, 3, 5, 4, 2, 7, 6   (Other answers are possible.)

3 Explain to the students that they represent an organisation that educates people about DRWH and helps people in the developing world design and make their own DRWH systems. To continue this work they must raise money from richer governments. Brainstorm how they can do this, e.g. using petitions, letter writing campaigns, etc.

4 Tell the students they are going to launch an e-mail campaign. They must write the text of the e-mail which supporters of DRHW can download from a website and send to their own governments. Brainstorm the characteristics of such an e-mail. It will be formal, concise and have an opening and closing formula, e.g. *Dear Sir or Madam / Yours faithfully* or *Dear (name) / Yours sincerely*, and it will make use of set phrases that express opinion, e.g. *We believe …, There's no doubt …, Clearly, …,* etc. You may want to give students a copy of Writing organisation 2 to help them with this (see p.124). Discuss how the paragraphs should be structured and ordered, i.e.: *What the project is; Why it is needed; What you want from your country's government; How the donor government will benefit*.

5 In pairs, tell the students they have ten minutes to write the e-mail, being as persuasive as possible and using facts from the Water Facts.

6 After ten minutes, ask them to swap their e-mail with another pair, read the other pair's e-mail and feedback on how well the arguments are put and whether they feel it would persuade the government to act.

Follow up

- Ask the students to write the text of an e-mail for a similar campaign on an issue which they feel strongly about.

- Ask the students to write an article for a website introducing the e-mail campaign. This should include a headline, a brief description of the organisation and the campaign and a paragraph on what you should do with the e-mail once you have downloaded it.

Domestic Rain Water Harvesting (DRWH)

A system for collecting water for drinking, cooking and washing

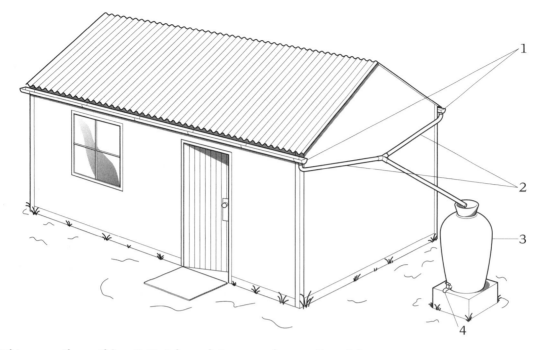

Where are these things? Match each to a number on the picture:

storage tank ....

down pipes ....

guttering ....

outlet tap ....

Water Facts

People need to harvest rain water in places like South Asia, East Africa and Central America because:

1 Thousands of people die from preventable diseases like diarrhoea, typhoid and dysentery caught from dirty ground water.

2 With a good filter or boiling, stored rain water is safe to drink.

3 Millions of people, mainly women and children, have to walk many kilometres to collect water.

4 DRWH can supply the home with clean water for 50–90% of the year.

5 Digging wells is only a partial answer; some ground water supplies are becoming polluted, others are drying up.

6 People are more likely to take care of their own domestic storage tank than a larger communal one.

7 Guttering and storage tanks can be made locally from cheap materials.

Writing tool kit

This section contains a variety of integrated photocopiable reference materials that can be used with your students to help improve their writing skills. These are explicitly exploited in some lessons and are also provided as a means of extending the writing focus beyond the one-off lesson. The materials are:

First draft checklist / correction code – helps students to improve first drafts

Second draft checklist / correction code – helps students to improve second drafts

First draft correction: examples – helps students to use the First draft checklist / correction code: consists of a draft business letter, which has been annotated using the correction code, and a corrected version of the same letter

Second draft correction: examples – helps students to use the Second draft checklist / correction code: consists of typical technical and mechanical errors, annotated using the correction code, and their corrections

Writing organisation 1 and **2** – a quick reference to help students plan and check organisation (re: First draft checklist)

Writing style 1 and **2** – a quick reference to help students check style (re: First draft checklist)

Teacher's writing evaluation scale – helps teachers evaluate/grade students' work: consists of two separate scales based on the First and Second draft checklists

Student writing evaluation chart – helps students request specific feedback based on the First and Second draft checklists

Useful potential resources: writing websites and files

How to use the checklists

The drafting checklists and correction codes (along with the evaluation scale and chart) can be used on their own, or combined to form an integrated set of revising tools. By emphasising the *process* of writing, they help the student differentiate between a work in progress and the finished product. The student learns to analyse and correct their own errors during writing, rather than after a piece has been 'completed' and evaluated by the teacher, and so becomes a more self-critical, confident and independent writer.

To help this self-correction and redrafting, you may wish to encourage students to write their first drafts on alternate lines of lined paper.

First draft checklist / correction code

This focuses on global errors (communication, organisation, layout and style) that impede understanding. Students use the checklist questions to identify problems with the draft, and the code to mark on the draft where these problems are. They can use the questions in the checklist in several ways:

– to help analyse how effective their own first drafts are at communicating what they want to say.

– to form the basis of a conference/discussion with another student, or the teacher.

– to check other students' work, using the code to mark any areas that they feel need reworking to aid understanding.

The annotated first draft is then returned to the writer to form the basis of discussion and/or a new draft.

Second draft checklist / correction code

This focuses on technical and mechanical errors (grammar, vocabulary, punctuation and spelling) which can sometimes impede communication. Once students have revised any global errors and written a second draft, they can use this checklist and the correction codes in exactly the same way as the First draft checklist.

First draft correction: examples

This gives examples of the types of global errors that are highlighted by the First draft checklist, and how the codes can be applied. It also shows the corrected/model version. You could enlarge a copy to A3 and display it in the classroom to act as a reference for students. Alternatively, you may wish to give them all a copy to use when they are revising their own annotated first drafts. For lower level students you may want to write your own version of this, using just the code **1→2** to indicate organisational problems and **st** for style.

Second draft correction: examples

This gives examples of the types of technical or mechanical errors that are highlighted by the Second draft checklist. This can be used in the same way as the First draft correction: examples sheet. For lower level students you may want to write your own version of this, using just these symbols: **Gr, WO, ^, /, Voc, P, Sp.**

Some ideas for introducing the checklists

- Comparing checklists:

  1 Make one copy of Letter 1 from Unit 15.2 per pair of students. In pairs, give half the pairs copies of the First draft checklist and the other half copies of the Second draft checklist.

  2 Ask the pairs to discuss the text using their checklist questions and to identify what they think are the five most important errors but not correct them. Divide the board in half.

  3 After ten minutes, feedback onto the board, putting global errors on the left and technical/mechanical errors on the right. Brainstorm which most impede communication and should thus be tackled first when redrafting (i.e. global errors). At this stage, you may wish to brainstorm corrections.

- Identifying errors:

  1 In pairs, give each pair a copy of a text containing errors and a copy of one of either of the checklists. Ask them to read the text and identify the errors but not mark them on it.

  2 Tell them to place a blank sheet of paper alongside the text and, using the checklists, write appropriate questions/comments on the paper alongside each error. When they have had sufficient time, ask them to join with another pair and swap their pieces of paper.

3 Ask them to compare their questions/comments and discuss why they chose those particular ones.

This way of using checklists encourages conferencing and leaves the original student's draft unmarked, and can, therefore, be less threatening.

Some ideas for introducing the correction codes

Lower level students:
Write a short text on the board containing only one or two types of error, e.g. spelling and vocabulary. Ask the students to identify the types of error and annotate them using the simplified code.

Higher level students:
- Make one copy of the First draft correction: examples for each pair of students. Cut off the Answer key. Give each pair a copy of the code without the key. Ask them to compare the model business letter with the first draft, identify how it differs and discuss what they think the different codes mean. When they have had sufficient time, give each pair a copy of the code to check their predictions.

- Make one copy of the Second draft correction: examples. Use correction fluid to blank out the corrections. Photocopy one copy of your altered code per pair of students. In pairs, tell them to write their own corrections. Feedback as a whole class.

- Make one copy of Letter 1 from Unit 15.2 and underline the errors. Make one copy of this amended letter per pair of students. In pairs, ask them to annotate the copy using the correction code from the First draft checklist, but not correct it. When they have done this, ask them to join with another pair and check their annotations. Tell the pairs to swap their letters and redraft them. When they have had sufficient time, ask them to swap back and follow the same procedure, this time using the correction code from the Second draft checklist.

- In pairs, ask each student to copy out a different short text (possibly from their coursebook) and add five different deliberate errors. Tell them to swap their text with their partner, identify the five errors and use the correction code from the Second draft checklist to annotate them. When the students have had sufficient time, ask them to check their answers with their partner.

- Error sale:
  1 Write a text that includes all the different types of errors in the correction code from the Second draft checklist. In groups of four, give each group a copy of the text. Ask them to read the text together and mark it using the correction code.

  2 When they have had sufficient time, stop them and tell them you are going to buy their errors. Write the code for one error, e.g. *Voc* on the board and ask the first group for an example from the text. If they give a good example, award them 100 euros.

  3 Write a different code on the board and repeat the procedure with the second group. Continue until all fifteen codes have been covered. The group with the most euros at the end is the winner!

Writing tool kit

First draft checklist / correction code

Students: use this to help you check and correct your first draft.

Communication	Code
How easy is it to understand? Does anything need to be made clearer?	
Does the reader have all the information they need?	?
Is there too much information? Have you used too many words?	/
Has any information been repeated?	Rep
How enjoyable or useful is it?	☺ or ☺ ☺ or ☺ ☺ ☺
Organisation	
Have you organised the information and ideas logically?	1→2
Have you used paragraphs, sections or headings to help the reader?	Par
Are they clearly linked using discourse markers? e.g. *however, although,* etc.	Link
Is the opening appropriate? Does it make the reader want to read more?	Start
Does it end in the right place?	End
Layout	
Have you used the right layout for this type of writing?	L
Style	
How formal or informal is this type of writing? Is this appropriate? Is this descriptive enough or too descriptive for this type of writing? Would the passive or the active form be more appropriate?	St

From *Writing Extra* by Graham Palmer © Cambridge University Press 2004 **PHOTOCOPIABLE**

 -

Second draft checklist / correction code

Students: use this to help you check and correct your second draft.

Grammar	Code
Have you used the right verb forms?	V
Do the subject and verb agree in each sentence? Is the subject missing?	Sub
Are the words in the right order?	WO
Have you used the right prepositions?	Prep
Have you checked the nouns? Are they uncountable? Are they plural?	N
Have you used the right article?	Art
Have you used the right structure?	Gr
Have you only split a word at the end of a syllable?	Syll
Have you missed out any words?	^
Have you used too many words?	/
Vocabulary	
Have you used the right word? Is it positive, negative or neutral?	Voc
Can you use a specific word not a general one? Is it too weak or strong?	Gen
Punctuation	
Does the punctuation make the writing easy to understand?	P
Have you used capital letters in the right place?	Cap
Spelling	
Have you checked difficult words are spelt correctly?	Sp

 From *Writing Extra* by Graham Palmer © Cambridge University Press 2004 **PHOTOCOPIABLE**

First draft correction: examples

Students: use this to help you correct your first drafts.

Corrected letter

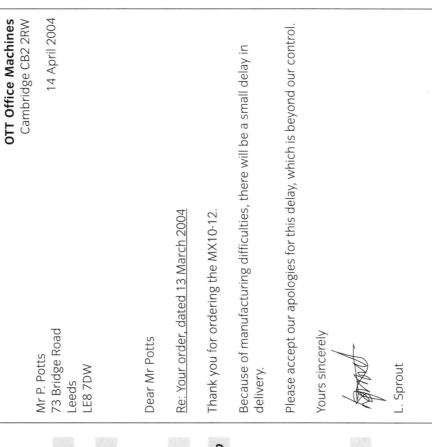

OTT Office Machines
Cambridge CB2 2RW
14 April 2004

Mr P. Potts
73 Bridge Road
Leeds
LE8 7DW

Dear Mr Potts

Re: Your order, dated 13 March 2004

Thank you for ordering the MX10-12.

Because of manufacturing difficulties, there will be a small delay in delivery.

Please accept our apologies for this delay, which is beyond our control.

Yours sincerely

L. Sprout

7 St   **8 ?**   **9 /**   **10 Rep**   **11 L**

First draft of letter (with errors)

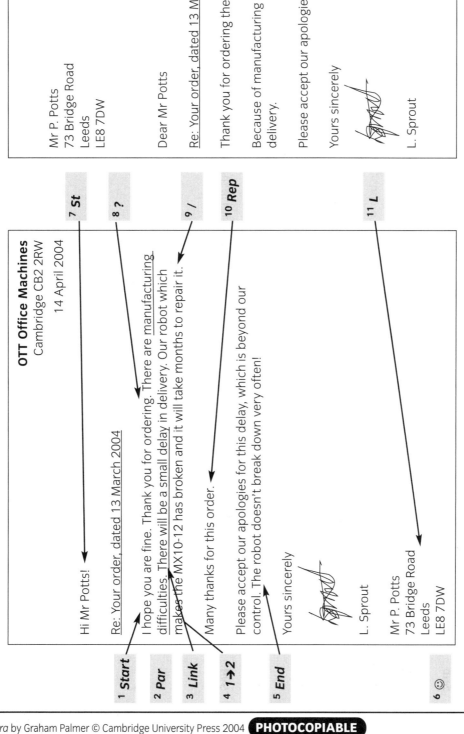

OTT Office Machines
Cambridge CB2 2RW
14 April 2004

Hi Mr Potts!

Re: Your order, dated 13 March 2004

I hope you are fine. Thank you for ordering. There are manufacturing difficulties. There will be a small delay in delivery. Our robot which makes the MX10-12 has broken and it will take months to repair it.

Many thanks for this order.

Please accept our apologies for this delay, which is beyond our control. The robot doesn't break down very often!

Yours sincerely

L. Sprout

Mr P. Potts
73 Bridge Road
Leeds
LE8 7DW

1 Start   **2 Par**   **3 Link**   **4 1→2**   **5 End**   **6 ☺**

Answer key

1 The opening is not appropriate **2** Split into paragraphs **3** Join these sentences **4** Arrange these ideas logically **5** This is not a good way to finish **6** This letter communicates but not very well **7** This is too informal **8** This is confusing: what has he ordered? **9** Cut this **10** This repeats information **11** This address is in the wrong place

Writing tool kit

Second draft correction: examples

Students: use this to help you correct your second drafts.

Code	Typical error	Explanation	Correction
V	He work in Tokyo.	You need a different form of the verb.	He works in Tokyo.
Sub	Is very exciting.	The subject is missing.	It is very exciting.
WO	Is very exciting my job.	The words are in the wrong order.	My job is very exciting.
Prep	He was looking to a postcard.	You need a different preposition.	He was looking at a postcard.
N	I have got two child.	You need the plural noun.	I have got two children.
Art	My office is in city centre.	You have used the wrong article or an article is missing.	My office is in the city centre.
Gr	I enjoy to dance.	You have made a grammar mistake.	I enjoy dancing.
Syll	My parents live in a big apar-tment.	You have split the word in the wrong place.	My parents live in a big apart-ment.
^	I want learn English.	A word is missing.	I want to learn English.
/	I come from in Turkey.	There are too many words.	I come from Turkey.
Voc	He is a management.	You have used the wrong word.	He is a manager.
Gen	He was talking so I couldn't hear him.	You could use a more specific word.	He was whispering.
P	I want a good job more money and children.	You need some punctuation.	I want a good job, more money and children.
Cap	I have many plans for the Future.	You do not need a capital letter.	I have many plans for the future.
Sp	I am studing English at university.	You have spelt something wrong.	I am studying English at university.

From *Writing Extra* by Graham Palmer © Cambridge University Press 2004 **PHOTOCOPIABLE**

Writing organisation 1

Students: use this as a quick reference when you are planning your writing and checking its structure. (See also the First draft checklist.)

Planning

Brainstorm ideas and information onto a mind map:

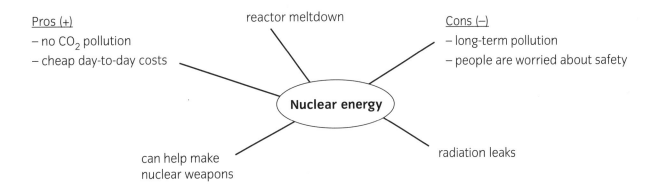

Answer some or all of these questions in your writing: *Who? What? When? Where? How? Why?*

Structure the ideas and information appropriately, e.g.

Formal letter Greeting (*Dear …*) Reason for writing More details What should happen next Close (*Yours …*)	**Fiction** Introduction: the main problem Partial answer to the problem The answer creates a new problem Final answer
Discursive composition Introduction Most important point Second most important point Third most important point, etc. Conclusion/Summary	**Business report** Summary Introduction Prioritised points Conclusion Recommendations

Checking structure

Make sure you use a new paragraph for each new topic or for when something changes in a story, e.g. location, time or the character you are focusing on. Check that each paragraph starts by focusing on specifics and then expands into the more general, e.g.

> Topic sentence giving the main idea of the paragraph ➜ Sentences giving details, examples, comparisons, etc. ➜ Final sentence restating the main idea of the paragraph.

Make sure you use pronouns, e.g. *this, that, he, she,* etc. to refer to things you have already mentioned. Check that the reader can easily understand what each pronoun refers to, e.g.

> The house has three bedrooms. *It* is in a beautiful little village near Stratford.

Make sure you use discourse markers, e.g. *however, certainly, on the whole,* etc. to link your ideas together. (See also Writing organisation 2.)

Writing organisation 2

Students: use this as a quick reference when you check that your ideas are linked together logically. (See also the First draft checklist.) If you find more discourse markers as you study, add them to this list under the correct heading.

Useful words and phrases – discourse markers

Adding a new point	Maria is a hard worker. She is *also* very experienced. Maria is a hard worker. *Furthermore*, she is very experienced. *As well as / In addition to* being a hard worker, Maria is very experienced.
Adding a similar point	E-mail is useful if you need an answer quickly. *Similarly / In the same way*, mobile phones make it easier to keep in touch.
Referring to a previous point	*With reference to* Mr Pearson's mistake, I do not think it will happen again. *As far as* Mr Pearson's mistake *is concerned*, I do not think …
Clarifying a point	The car was a good buy. *That is to say / In other words*, we have had no problems with it since we bought it.
Showing how two points contrast	He is intelligent *but* he does not understand the system. *Although* he is intelligent, he does not understand the system. *In spite of / Despite being* intelligent, he does not … He is intelligent. *However/Nevertheless*, he does not … *While/Whereas* I think you are mostly right, I disagree with some points.
Strongly agreeing with a point	*Certainly / Of course*, new employees need training.
Strongly disagreeing with a point	You state that nuclear power is cheap. *On the contrary*, it is very expensive.
Showing a logical result	Older people must be good to children. *In this way/Thus*, children will learn to be good. The politician was very unpopular. *So/Therefore/Consequently / As a result*, he was not elected.
Showing a sequence	*First*, we must invest in developing the product. *Next*, we must train our sales people. *Finally*, we must sell, sell, sell!
Generalising	*On the whole/In general*, our products are popular.
Giving examples	*For example / For instance*, the MX25 computer sells well.
Summarising	*In brief / In conclusion / To sum up*, our sales are improving.

Writing style 1

Students: use this as a quick reference when you check the style of your piece of writing. (See also the First draft checklist.)

Informal or neutral (personal) style

Who? *People you know well.*
Why? *To show closeness/friendliness.*
Where? *Personal e-mail, letters, etc.*

Grammar

Use immediate tenses: simple/present
I *want* to ask about …
I *wonder* if you can …

Use direct statements
I need you to swap this for another one.

Use direct requests and questions
Please phone me.
How did you lose my order?

Use modals can *and* will
Can you do this?
Will you come to my party?

Use contractions
I can't understand it.

Use ellipsis (leaving out words)
The computer ~~which~~ I bought from you doesn't work.

Vocabulary

Use everyday language, e.g.
ask about (something)
ask for (something)
buy (something)
say sorry (for something)
swap (something)
tell (someone something)
think about (something)
write to / phone (someone)

Formal (impersonal) style

Who? *Strangers and people you do not know well.*
Why? *To show distance/respect.*
Where? *Business e-mail, letters and reports; newspaper articles, etc.*

Grammar

Use less immediate tenses: continuous/past
I *am writing* to enquire about …
I *was wondering* if you could …

Use conditional statements
I would be grateful, *if* you could exchange this.

Use less direct requests; yes/no questions
Could you please contact me?
Could you explain how you lost my order?

Use modals could *and* would
Could you do this?
Would you come to my party?

No contractions
I cannot understand it.

No ellipsis
The computer *which* I bought from you does not work.

Vocabulary

Avoid idioms/slang. Use specific vocabulary, e.g.
enquire about (something)
request (something)
purchase (something)
apologise (for something)
exchange (something)
inform/advise (someone)
consider (something)
contact (someone)

Writing style 2

Students: use this sheet as a quick reference when you need to think of a more formal style for a phrase. (See also the First draft checklist.) If you find more useful informal/formal equivalent phrases as you study, add them to the list under the correct heading.

Informal or neutral (personal) style		Formal (impersonal) style
Hi/Dear Paula ➜ *Bye for now! / Best wishes*	**Greeting ➜ Closing**	*Dear Ms/Mrs/Miss/Mr Johnson* ➜ *Yours sincerely* *Dear Sir or Madam* ➜ *Yours faithfully*
Please can you …	**Asking**	*I would be grateful if you could …*
Can I send you a brochure?	**Offering**	*Would you like me to forward a brochure?*
No, thanks!	**Refusing**	*Thank you for your offer but I am afraid I have to refuse.*
Thanks. That will be great!	**Accepting**	*I would be (very) happy to accept …*
Thanks a lot. / Cheers!	**Thanking**	*I am (extremely) grateful for …*
I've had enough of this noise!	**Complaining**	*I wish to make a (serious) complaint about the noise.*
I'm sorry.	**Apologising**	*Please accept my (sincere) apologies.*
I think that …	**Stating opinion**	*It is possible that …*
I'm sure that …	**Stating fact**	*It is (absolutely) certain that …*
Do you mean that …?	**Checking**	*Could you clarify that …?*
You're right that …	**Agreeing**	*I would (completely) agree that …*
You're wrong that …	**Disagreeing**	*(I am afraid) I cannot agree that …*
Well done!	**Congratulating**	*Please accept my congratulations.*
I'm so sorry (for you).	**Commiserating**	*I do sympathise.*

From *Writing Extra* by Graham Palmer © Cambridge University Press 2004   **PHOTOCOPIABLE**

Teacher's writing evaluation scale

Teachers: use this to standardise marking across different writing forms. It can be used to give a general grade (out of ten) or a more detailed (%) grade. You may want to display a copy so that students can see what their grades mean and where they need to improve.

General Grades (out of ten)

Task (5) + Language (5) = 10

Detailed Grades (out of 100)

Communication (5) + organisation (5) + layout (5) + style (5) + grammar (5) + vocabulary (5) + punctuation (5) + spelling (5) = (40) x 2.5 = % grade

Grade		Task
Very poor	1	**Communication**: This is very difficult to understand. **Organisation**: Your ideas are disorganised. **Layout**: You have not used the correct layout for this type of writing. **Style**: You have not used the correct level of formality.
Poor	2	**Communication**: This is difficult to understand. **Organisation**: Some of your ideas are organised logically. **Layout**: You have used the correct layout but with a lot of errors. **Style**: You have used the correct level of formality but with a lot of errors.
Average	3	**Communication**: I can understand this. **Organisation**: Your ideas are organised. **Layout**: You have used the correct layout with some errors. **Style**: You have used the correct level of formality with some errors.
Good	4	**Communication**: This is easy to understand. **Organisation**: Your ideas are well organised. **Layout**: You have used the correct layout with a few errors. **Style**: You have used the correct level of formality with a few errors.
Very good	5	**Communication**: This is very easy to understand. **Organisation**: Your ideas are very well organised. **Layout**: You have used the correct layout. **Style**: You have used the correct level of formality.

Grade		Language
Very poor	1	**Grammar**: You do not use simple structures correctly. **Vocabulary**: You do not use the right vocabulary. **Punctuation**: Your punctuation and use of capital letters is very weak. **Spelling**: Your spelling is very weak.
Poor	2	**Grammar**: You use some simple structures correctly. **Vocabulary**: You use some of the right vocabulary. **Punctuation**: Your punctuation and use of capital letters is weak. **Spelling**: Your spelling is weak.
Average	3	**Grammar**: You use simple structures correctly but not complicated ones. **Vocabulary**: You use a range of the right vocabulary. **Punctuation**: Your punctuation and use of capital letters has some errors. **Spelling**: Your spelling has some errors.
Good	4	**Grammar**: You use complicated structures correctly with a few errors. **Vocabulary**: You use a good range of vocabulary. **Punctuation**: Your punctuation and use of capital letters is good. **Spelling**: Your spelling is good.
Very good	5	**Grammar**: You use complicated structures correctly. **Vocabulary**: You use a very good range of vocabulary. **Punctuation**: Your punctuation and use of capital letters is very good. **Spelling**: Your spelling is very good.

Student writing evaluation chart

Students: use this when you have written a draft to say what you want checked or when you have finished a piece of writing to say what you want graded.

Name	TASK				LANGUAGE				
	Communication	Organisation	Layout	Style	Grammar	Vocabulary	Punctuation	Spelling	Everything (Total)
Tick the areas you want checked									
Grade	5	5	5	5	5	5	5	5	40

Total x 2.5 = Detailed % grade

From *Writing Extra* by Graham Palmer © Cambridge University Press 2004 **PHOTOCOPIABLE**

- -

How to use the Student writing evaluation chart

This can be used in conjunction with the Teacher's writing evaluation scale to give students control of the evaluation process.

For each finished piece of writing, give students a copy of this chart and ask them to tick what they want graded. For example, if they have used the Second draft checklist to improve their language, they may want to be graded only on grammar.

This chart can also be used during the drafting stages. In this case, no grading is done. Instead, the student ticks the areas they want feedback on and the teacher, or another student, then uses the chart to focus on areas to correct in the draft. Any changes can then form the basis for discussion with the original writer.

Useful potential resources: writing websites and files

You or your students may want to visit these websites to discover more useful resources:

http://owl.english.purdue.edu/ (an online writing lab)

http://www.managementhelp.org/commskls/cmm_writ.htm (a business writers' library)

http://dictionary.cambridge.org/ (an online dictionary)

You may also want to build up a Resource file containing varying samples of different genres which your students can refer to. When you publish their work in school magazines, in displays on class notice boards or on an Internet class home page, also photocopy the best pieces and file them according to genre in the class Resource file.

Ask students to keep their own individual writing files divided in three sections: drafts, finished writing, and evaluations. The third section can include writing journals, reports on how they wrote a piece, and evaluations made by themselves and their teacher using the Teacher's writing evaluation scale.